DA BULL
Life Over The Edge

DA BULL
Life Over The Edge

by
GREG NOLL
and
ANDREA GABBARD

North Atlantic Books
Berkeley, California

ISBN 1-55643-143-0

Published by
North Atlantic Books
P.O. Box 12327
Berkeley, CA 94712

Cover photo by John Severson. Courtesy *Surfer* Magazine.
Back cover serigraph, "Makaha," by Ken Auster, originally published by Marco Fine Arts. Courtesy of the artist.

Printed in the United States of America by Malloy Lithographing

DA BULL: Life Over The Edge is sponsored by the Society for the Study of Native Arts and Sciences, a nonprofit educational corporation whose goals are to develop an educational and crosscultural perspective linking various scientific, social, and artistic fields; to nurture a holistic view of the arts, sciences, humanities, and healing; and to publish and distribute literature on the relationship of mind, body, and nature.

This book is dedicated to Laura.

*It is not so much that I got
there from here, which is everyone's
story: but the shape
of the voyage, how it pushed
outward in every direction . . .*

Jim Harrison

CONTENTS

Acknowledgments

PREFACE

I've never met Greg Noll. So I know no more about him than you might before reading this book. Apparently, not many people knew much about Greg Noll. The big-wave surfers of the fifties and sixties, his peers, fellow pioneers, knew he was . . . the best? No. It's a slight to the others who were in the lineup with him, day after day, year after year, to say any one of them was best. As surfers are individuals, so are their styles on the water, and how do you compare such a thing as style? Along with beauty, "best" is in the eye of the beholder.

Most of the surfers who were there to behold Greg Noll, however, agree that he was the best at being brave.

Over the last twenty years, as a senior writer and special contributor to *Sports Illustrated,* I've written about many brave men. Most of them have been motor racers: motorcycles, cars, powerboats and airplanes. But there have also been speed skiers, mountain climbers and big-wave surfers. It's interesting to compare their drives and motivations. There are similarities, such as the control of fear. And there are parallels: the joy that comes from meeting a high-risk challenge and overcoming it with skill and a steady psyche. Between racers and surfers, though, there is at least one big difference. Greg Noll explains it succinctly: "You have to love what you're doing to go out there and do it when the bleachers are empty." And when your life is on the line, for free.

Big-wave surfers are more like big-wall climbers. New walls were being discovered and climbed in Yosemite Valley about the same time that big waves on Oahu were first being ridden, and in both cases it was the brave pioneers of a pure sport who were "expanding the envelope," as a test pilot might say. What burning ambition motivated them? Yvon Chouinard, who today owns the Patagonia outdoor clothing company, was one of the early leaders of big-wall climbing. Chouinard had a name for what he and his pioneer buddies were: "Fun hogs."

Listen to Greg Noll again: "Those of us who began surfing during that era are considered to be pioneers, but I think none of us had any sense of history about what we were doing. We were having fun."

Simple, complete fun, nonstop whenever possible. It was the pilot flame of ambition burning inside those early big-wave surfers. Rising from the blaze were smoky tentacles of emotions that were more complicated, of course, but those emotions were not what propelled these men out to the lineup. They are also another story.

Greg Noll's era on the big waves is gone. But the waves remain. Ricky Grigg, who still lives on Oahu and rides them, points out that the clock *can* be turned back: early of a morning, on a day when the hordes of modern surfers might be somewhere else on the island, someplace where the bleachers are full. On those days, it can almost be as it was. The same Waimea twenty-footer. The same board. The same comfortable isolation waiting for the wave, and familiar butterflies watching it come, the exhilaration of shooting down its face, and the memorable oneness when you become a part of it. The only difference is that no legends will be created this day.

No big deal. What does legend-making have to do with joy anyhow?

You won't find the word "nostalgia" used much in this book. Greg Noll isn't here to tell you, "Ah, those were the days." You get to decide that for yourself, just as you get to decide for yourself about Greg Noll's motivation—he's not a blabbering kind of man. He was, however, persuaded to sit down and tell you what those days, and that special time, were like.

As Ricky Grigg says about the riders of big waves: "It's like old bullfighters getting together. What's important is not how fast the bull is running; it's how it feels when he misses you by an inch. That's the story, isn't it?"

That is the story. Turn the page and begin.

Sam Moses
Summerland Key, Florida
June, 1989

I analyzed the situation a little longer and gave myself better than a fifty-percent chance of surviving one of these monsters. I just figured I had an edge, since all my surfing had been devoted to big waves. My motivation was also competitive. Deep down inside I had always wanted to catch a bigger wave than anyone else had ever ridden. Now, here was my chance. After a lifetime of working up to it, the time had finally come to either shit or get off the pot. The chances of this type of surf occurring again might be another eleven or twelve years away, and out of my grasp.

Even though I had put a lot of time into riding big waves, I knew there was no chance of actually riding one of those waves all the way through. Not the way they were folding over in such huge sections. The best I could expect would be to get down the face to the bottom of the wave, make my turn, then put it in high gear and get as far as I could before the whole thing folded over on me. Then I'd have to take my chances on the swim in. Getting in would be half the danger—if I survived the impact zone, I'd have to fight my way through that strong side current and into the beach before I reached the rocky shoreline.

By this time the crowd in the water had thinned way down. I paddled about fifty yards away from the other guys to sit and do some more thinking. That's my whole deal. I can wait. Like Peter Cole and Pat Curren, I've always been willing to wait for the bigger sets. I always preferred to wait it out, catch fewer waves but, I hoped, bigger ones.

Everyone else had paddled in. It felt very lonely out there, but I was working on an adrenalin high. A lot of conflicts were racing around in my head. My chance of a lifetime—am I going to blow it or do something about it? I've got a family, kids and people I care about a great deal—is this goddamn wave really worth risking my life? I felt kind of crazy even considering it.

What it came down to was that I realized that I'd come all this way, all these years, for this moment. This "Makaha magic" was only going to happen once in my lifetime and that time was *now*. The next time it happened I'd either be hobbling around on a cane or dead of old age. In either case, I'd forever miss my one chance to catch a wave this large.

I've always had one kind of approach to surfing big waves. That is "Don't hesitate. Once you decide to go, *go*. Don't screw around." You get into more trouble trying to change your mind midstream—or midwave—than you do if you just make a commitment and go for it.

6

was one of the early leaders of big-wall climbing. Chouinard had a name for what he and his pioneer buddies were: "Fun hogs."

Listen to Greg Noll again: "Those of us who began surfing during that era are considered to be pioneers, but I think none of us had any sense of history about what we were doing. We were having fun."

Simple, complete fun, nonstop whenever possible. It was the pilot flame of ambition burning inside those early big-wave surfers. Rising from the blaze were smoky tentacles of emotions that were more complicated, of course, but those emotions were not what propelled these men out to the lineup. They are also another story.

Greg Noll's era on the big waves is gone. But the waves remain. Ricky Grigg, who still lives on Oahu and rides them, points out that the clock *can* be turned back: early of a morning, on a day when the hordes of modern surfers might be somewhere else on the island, someplace where the bleachers are full. On those days, it can almost be as it was. The same Waimea twenty-footer. The same board. The same comfortable isolation waiting for the wave, and familiar butterflies watching it come, the exhilaration of shooting down its face, and the memorable oneness when you become a part of it. The only difference is that no legends will be created this day.

No big deal. What does legend-making have to do with joy anyhow?

You won't find the word "nostalgia" used much in this book. Greg Noll isn't here to tell you, "Ah, those were the days." You get to decide that for yourself, just as you get to decide for yourself about Greg Noll's motivation—he's not a blabbering kind of man. He was, however, persuaded to sit down and tell you what those days, and that special time, were like.

As Ricky Grigg says about the riders of big waves: "It's like old bullfighters getting together. What's important is not how fast the bull is running; it's how it feels when he misses you by an inch. That's the story, isn't it?"

That is the story. Turn the page and begin.

Sam Moses
Summerland Key, Florida
June, 1989

INTRODUCTION

Surfing's popularity goes way back, centuries ago, to the ancient Hawaiians. The sport played an important role in early Hawaiian culture, both as competition and as part of harvest celebrations. Hawaiian royalty used wooden planks hewn of koa and breadfruit trees to ride waves off places such as Kalehuawehe (Waikiki) and Pau Malu (Sunset Beach).

In the eighteenth century, with the coming of the missionaries, traditional Hawaiian culture began to fade and surfing went into limbo. In the early 1900s, Duke Kahanamoku, a Hawaiian who became famous for his feats as an Olympic swimmer, injected life back into the sport and eventually introduced it to the Mainland. Surfers rode waves on heavy redwood planks up to eighteen feet long until after World War II, when a few enthusiasts began experimenting with lighter materials such as balsa. Today's surfers navigate on sticks of lightweight foam and fiberglass through a liquid world that has not changed since the days of the Ancients. It's a world where you quickly learn that the only rules that exist are the ones that Mother Nature makes up—you're just along for the ride.

Tales of surfing feats date to the days of the original Hawaiians. The telling of surf stories rivals the telling of fish stories—that is, the details often grow in proportion to the number of times the story is told. In fishing, the size of the fish grows with each telling. In surfing, it's the size of the wave.

There are exceptions. Sometimes you catch a big one that doesn't need inflating. It's already big enough. Maybe it's too big.

Each winter, surfers from all over the world who dream of riding big surf migrate to Hawaii. The Hawaiian Islands happen to be perfectly situated in the path of immense swells created by storms off the Aleutian

Islands in Alaska. By the time they hit the island of Oahu, the swells can produce ridable waves up to thirty feet—or bigger—at well-known surf spots such as Waimea Bay, Sunset Beach, the outside reefs at Pipeline and Makaha Point.

During the winter of '69, the swells that rolled down from the Aleutian Islands to the North Shore left some memorable days in their wake. On December 4, these mountainous swells closed down the North Shore and reached around to Makaha Point, on the other side of Oahu. That day, the waves were too big for all but a fraction of surfers who made up the league of big-wave riders.

The growing swells eventually forced all but one big-wave rider back to shore. Greg Noll stayed out at Makaha to confront a massive, liquid force that had beckoned but eluded him for twenty years.

Like other sports that engender heroic feats, the sport of big-wave riding has spawned many legends. Noll is one. The men he talks about are others. Just as we may not understand why the mountain climber lives to climb Mt. Everest—the famous saying, "Because it's there," just doesn't satisfy—we also may not understand why big-wave riders live to catch the biggest wave. Unlike a mountain, a giant peak of moving water is not always there.

Noll spent all of his surfing years in pursuit of the biggest wave. During early discussions about this biography, he was hesitant to talk about it. "Talk is bullshit," he said. "You want to know the truth? Get a board and paddle out there, point your board down the face of a grinder and make a commitment. That's where you find the truth."

Noll's bullheaded approach to riding big waves didn't go unnoticed by his fellow surfers. Phil Edwards, a man known as well for his grace and style on a surfboard as for his work in developing the Hobie Cat catamaran, tagged him Da Bull. Noll's size might also have contributed to the nickname. At six feet two and two hundred thirty pounds, Noll had a brawny surfing style that was based on straightforward power and determination. To this day, Peter Cole, one of the few surfers from Noll's era who still rides big waves, calls Noll "the gutsiest man I've ever known." Mike Stange, who followed Noll over the edge of some of the biggest waves ever ridden, calls him "the Babe Ruth of surfing."

Those who were there that day at Makaha, all big-wave riders in their own right, claim that Noll took off on the largest wave anyone has ever ridden. As it turned out, the police roadblocks, the distance of the swell from shore and the presumed scarcity of ridable surf prevented this historic day from being preserved on film. Maybe it's better that way, to leave it instead to surf legend, to be passed on from one surf generation to the next. One thing is certain: the size of the wave will not grow in the telling. It's already too big. And that's no bull.

Andrea Gabbard
Oakhurst, California
July, 1989

THE LAST WAVE

In many ways the winter of '69 was the peak of my life. I was thirty-two. I had a built a successful career of surfing and making surfboards. Although I had a wife and two sons, a ladyfriend named Laura had entered my life. That winter in the Islands happened to be the one trip that Laura made with me during that period. I'm glad she was there to share it with me. As it turned out, she became my lifelong companion and the mother of two of my children.

As usual, we stayed with Henry Preece in Haleiwa. I had stayed at Henry's house nearly every year, since I first met him and Buffalo Keaulana in the fifties, when I had first started coming to the Islands. Here I was, fifteen years later, still coming to the Islands each season for the big winter swell.

Henry's little wood-frame house is about four blocks from the water, where you can hear the surf and feel it when it gets big. About two o'clock one morning, I woke up to the sound of a far-off rumble, rumble, rumble and the rattle of dishes in the kitchen. Half asleep, I thought, "Hell of a time to run the tanks through." Every once in a while, the Army would drive its tanks down from Wahiawa, through Haleiwa and out to Kaena Point. I got up to take a whiz, and suddenly realized there were no tanks. It was the rumble of huge surf, breaking from the horizon.

I started pacing, tried to sleep, paced again. By sunrise my stomach was full of butterflies. My adrenalin was pumping. I was ready to go take a look at Waimea Bay. As soon as Laura and I got there, I could see that the whole North Shore was closed out. Solid whitewater as far as you could see. You can't go out when it gets that big. For the most part, on the very rare occasion when it gets that big, it's done all over the island.

Laura and I decided to go take a look at Makaha just for the hell of it. Every once in a while, when the North Shore closes out, Makaha Point still has ridable surf. Less often, when the North Shore closes out, Makaha does this wonderful, magical thing that I had heard about over the years from older surfers like George Downing and Buzzy Trent. If God sees fit to have that north swell come in at an absolute, perfect direction, Makaha gets unbelievably monstrous swells, as big or bigger than the ones that attack the North Shore, except they're not peak breaks. These Makaha giants peel off from the Point in precise, seemingly endless walls.

In the fifteen years that I had been coming to the Islands to surf, I had never seen Makaha do its magic. Sure, I had ridden a number of big Makaha Point days when the waves were breaking twenty feet, but compared to Waimea's hang-on-to-your-balls super-drop, Makaha Point surf just didn't have it for me. I had heard the stories. Supposedly the really huge surf at Makaha only happens about once every eleven or twelve years. I had missed the day in '58 when Buzzy Trent and George Downing rode some monster surf at Makaha. I was convinced that Waimea is where it's at. The ultimate go-for-broke spot. There's not a bigger place on the face of God's earth to ride than Waimea. That's the way it is and always will be, world without end.

Was I wrong!

Still, there was nothing to do on the North Shore, so we headed to Makaha, taking the road that led around Kaena Point. We figured the worst thing that could happen is that it would become a good excuse to see my old pal Buffalo, do a little beer drinking and talk stories Hawaiian-style.

Talking stories is part of surfing. Every surfer has stories to tell. I had started surfing when I was eleven years old and had heard a lot of stories from some of the great old board shapers, guys like Dale Velzy and Bob Simmons.

Simmons was one of the first to experiment with lightweight surf-boards. He was a Cal Tech engineer who was into competitive cycling before he ever heard of surfing. One day he got into a terrible accident on his bike—got hit by a car and went right through the windshield. Wracked up his arm. As it turns out, in the hospital he was put in a room next to a guy who surfed. This guy starts telling Simmons about surfing and Simmons gets real interested. This is how Simmons told the story:

2

"This guy tells me you take off on these waves and you start down the side and you angle off one way or the other and these waves throw out over the top of you. Suddenly you're inside this enclosure, a green room, and the wave has broken completely over you. If you want, you can yodel or yell and the noise bounces off the side of the walls. You go on like this for a while, then you go flying out of the other end of this tube into daylight."

Simmons' first indirect exposure to surfing really captivated him. He was determined to go out and get into that green room. He believed that every wave was like this, not realizing that it's every surfer's dream to spend even a second or two in that "green room."

I felt the intensity of twenty years of surfing bigger and bigger waves pent up inside me that day. As we approached Kaena Point we noticed several places where gigantic storm surf had already washed across the road. I told Laura to walk across the bad spots while I drove the car across. I held my door open, ready to bail out if a wave hit the car.

As soon as we reached Kaena Point, I knew this day was going to be different. Terrifying waves of fifty feet or bigger were pounding the end of the island. We stopped at a couple of places to take pictures. One memorable photo from that day shows a giant wave dwarfing a couple of beach shacks in the foreground. *Surfer* magazine printed it in its March 1970 issue with the description, "Kaena Point at forty, fifty, sixty or seventy feet." That day, the waves demolished several shacks on Kaena Point and nearby areas as well as a great portion of the road.

As we got nearer to Makaha Point, I said, "Holy shit. It's happening." Makaha was doing its magic.

Usually, no matter how big the north swell is, by the time it gets around to the Makaha side of the island, it dissipates or you're looking at full-on stormy, windy, nasty weather. The horizon off Maili Beach, south of Makaha, becomes what the old-timers call Maili cloudbreak. The rate of speed of big swells creates wind and spray that rains down on the ocean. On this day, the water was nearly as smooth as glass, beautiful, and the waves were so big that they literally put the fear of God in me.

The radio began to broadcast evacuation orders for people in homes on Makaha Point. The police had just started to put up barricades on the road, but we made it through and out to the Point. And there it was, not just ridable Makaha—great, big, horrifying Makaha.

I analyzed the situation a little longer and gave myself better than a fifty-percent chance of surviving one of these monsters. I just figured I had an edge, since all my surfing had been devoted to big waves. My motivation was also competitive. Deep down inside I had always wanted to catch a bigger wave than anyone else had ever ridden. Now, here was my chance. After a lifetime of working up to it, the time had finally come to either shit or get off the pot. The chances of this type of surf occurring again might be another eleven or twelve years away, and out of my grasp.

Even though I had put a lot of time into riding big waves, I knew there was no chance of actually riding one of those waves all the way through. Not the way they were folding over in such huge sections. The best I could expect would be to get down the face to the bottom of the wave, make my turn, then put it in high gear and get as far as I could before the whole thing folded over on me. Then I'd have to take my chances on the swim in. Getting in would be half the danger—if I survived the impact zone, I'd have to fight my way through that strong side current and into the beach before I reached the rocky shoreline.

By this time the crowd in the water had thinned way down. I paddled about fifty yards away from the other guys to sit and do some more thinking. That's my whole deal. I can wait. Like Peter Cole and Pat Curren, I've always been willing to wait for the bigger sets. I always preferred to wait it out, catch fewer waves but, I hoped, bigger ones.

Everyone else had paddled in. It felt very lonely out there, but I was working on an adrenalin high. A lot of conflicts were racing around in my head. My chance of a lifetime—am I going to blow it or do something about it? I've got a family, kids and people I care about a great deal—is this goddamn wave really worth risking my life? I felt kind of crazy even considering it.

What it came down to was that I realized that I'd come all this way, all these years, for this moment. This "Makaha magic" was only going to happen once in my lifetime and that time was *now*. The next time it happened I'd either be hobbling around on a cane or dead of old age. In either case, I'd forever miss my one chance to catch a wave this large.

I've always had one kind of approach to surfing big waves. That is "Don't hesitate. Once you decide to go, *go*. Don't screw around." You get into more trouble trying to change your mind midstream—or midwave—than you do if you just make a commitment and go for it.

6

I spent about half an hour going through this mental battle before I came to my decision: "I want to do this. It's worth it to me." Above all, if I let this moment slip by, I knew I would never forgive myself. As cornball as it sounds, this probably was as close to the moment of truth that I would ever get.

I paddled back to my lineup. I was oblivious to the fact that I was now the only guy left out there. All my thoughts were focused on catching *the wave*. The wave that might be my biggest and my last. Finally a set came thundering down that I thought looked pretty goddamn good. "O.K.," I said to myself, "let's give this thing a shot."

Every board I built for big waves was designed to catch waves. That meant that each board had to include three main things: length, flotation and ample scoop in the nose. The scoop enabled me to point the nose down the face of a wave and paddle hard without worrying about the nose catching a little water and causing me to hesitate. You can lose a good wave by having to pull back at the instant of takeoff, just to prevent the nose from going underwater. I wanted enough scoop in front so that when I laid that sonofabitch down and started grinding, I'd never have to hesitate.

Boards can do funny things at high speeds. If the board isn't shaped right, or the fin is set even slightly wrong, the board can track or catch an edge, sending you ass over teakettle. I was very familiar with my board. I had made it for big waves and used it for three seasons. For me it was the perfect big-wave board. At eleven feet, four inches long with a one-and-a-half-inch scoop in the nose, it was a big gun for big waves.

The first wave in the set looked huge. Something inside me said, "Let it go." As I paddled over the top of it, I caught a glimpse of my wave. It was even bigger. I turned and began paddling, hard. I felt a rush of adrenalin as the wave approached, lifted me and my board began to accelerate. Then I was on my feet, committed.

You could have stacked two eighteen-wheel semis on top of each other against the face of that wave and still have had room left over to ride it. I started down the front of the wave and my board began to howl like a goddamn jet. I had never heard it make that noise. I was going down the face of the wave so fast that air was getting trapped somewhere and the vibration was causing an ear-shattering *WHOOOOOOOOOOOO!*

I flew down the face, past the lip of the wave, and when I got to the bottom, which is where I wanted to be, I looked ahead and saw the sonofabitch starting to break in a section that stretched a block and a half in front of me. I started to lay back, thinking I could dig a hole and escape through the backside of the wave. The wave threw out a sheet of water over my head and engulfed me. Then for a split second the whole scene froze forever in my mind. There I was, in that liquid green room that Simmons had talked about so long ago. I had been in and out of this room many times. Only this time the room was bigger, more frightening, with the thunderous roar of the ocean bouncing off its walls. I realized I wasn't going to go flying out the other end into daylight. This time I was afraid there might be no way out.

My board flew out from under me. I hit the water going so fast that it felt like hitting concrete. I skidded on my back and looked up just as tons of whitewater exploded over me. It pounded me under. It thrashed and rolled me beneath the surface until my lungs burned and there was so much pressure that I felt my eardrums were going to burst. Just as I thought I would pass out, the whitewater finally began to dissipate and the turbulence released me. I made it to the surface, gulped for air and quickly looked outside. There was another monster, heading my way.

There have been many times at Waimea when I've lost my board while trying to catch a wave and had to dive deep to avoid getting caught by the whitewater, or soup, of the next wave. As a big wave passes overhead, it causes tremendous pressure to build in your ears and you have to pop them to clear it.

Here at Makaha I waited for each wave to get within fifty to seventy-five yards outside me, then I dove down about twenty feet and waited for it to pass. When the first wave broke overhead, I popped my ears and waited a couple of seconds before I heard the muffled sound of rumbling whitewater. The underwater turbulence of the giant wall of whitewater overhead caught me and thrashed me around. These waves were so big and there was so much soup in them that, each time I went under, the pain from the pressure in my ears was almost unbearable. In waves like these, if you can't equalize the pressure by popping your ears, you can lose an eardrum.

I figured the best I could do was try to remain oriented towards the surface and let the turbulence carry me away from the main break. By the time I had cleared the impact zone, the waves had carried me inward about three hundred yards. I started swimming hard for the Point.

I knew the current was bad and that my survival now depend[...] reaching the shore quickly. I reached for every ounce of strength I ha[...] I was still a hundred yards or so off the beach. I could see Clausmy[...] could see the rocky beach coming up. I was never a great swimmer, but on that day I had a real incentive to make it. I swam my ass off.

Even the shorebreak was breaking big. I kept thinking, "If I don't make it to the beach before the rocks, I'll have no place to come in. Did I go through all this hell just to lose it in the rocks?"

By now I was swimming almost parallel to the beach. I could see my good friend Buffalo in his lifeguard jeep, following me on shore. The current was so strong that the beach looked like it was smoking by me. I finally hit shore about fifty feet before the rocks began. I crawled up on the sand and flopped there on my stomach, just glad to be alive. Buff was there with the jeep and a cold beer. He got out, stood over me and shoved the beer in my face.

"Good ting you wen make 'em, Brudda," he said. "'Cause no way I was comin' in afta you. I was jus goin' wave goodbye and say 'Alooo-ha.'"

Other Recollections

LAURA

We had been watching Greg from on top of the empty judges' stand. After that wave wiped him out, we couldn't see him or his board. Everyone was saying he was gone. That's a strange feeling, hearing it all around you and not believing it. Not wanting to believe it.

I had been going with Greg then for about seven years. This was my first trip to the Islands. I knew that riding big waves was Greg's life, and I knew how strong he was in the water. It would never have occurred to me to say, "Don't go out."

It seemed like forever before someone with binoculars spotted his board, then spotted Greg. When I saw him swimming, I knew he'd make it.

Buff was throwing a big party that evening. Normally Greg would be up for a party, especially after a day of surfing. That day he just said no. He remained very quiet the rest of the day. It was a long time before he ever spoke of that day at Makaha.

———————

Excerpt from an article in *Honolulu Star-Bulletin,* Friday, December 5, 1969:

Storm Wave Wipes Out Champ Surfer

Greg Noll, one of the best of the big wave riders, yesterday came uncomfortably close to being a victim of Oahu's surf storm.

. . . About 1:30 p.m., Noll chose his challenge which another surfing champ, Fred Hemmings, described as "the biggest wave I've ever seen ridden."

But the ride came to an abrupt and terrifying halt only moments after it began. Noll was "wiped out and there I was straight under the wave and all I could see was a tiny patch of sunlight." Then he was tossed like a toothpick in the turbulent sea. . . .

Hemmings held his breath as he looked hard at the churning, "soupy" water for several long seconds before Noll's head reappeared. Hemmings said,

"The wave was too big. Too fast. Too massive. It was definitely a life or death situation. If it had been anyone else in that situation, he would have died."

Hemmings said having that size wave "explode" as it did on Noll is akin to having a "giant Wall of China falling on you."

———————

My board survived that day. I still have it hanging in my garage. The image of getting buried in Simmons' green room remains very clear in my mind. I know that any surfer who has been in that green room never forgets it. I also know that if you screw around with it long enough, you'll get to know it intimately. It might be the last room you're ever in.

I don't know how big the wave was. I will say that it was at least ten feet bigger than anything I had surfed at Waimea Bay and far more dangerous. There were people there who saw it. Everyone has an opinion of how big it was. I'd like to leave it at that.

After I had analyzed what I'd done, I asked myself, "You're not going to top that, so where do you go from here? What do you do now?"

I didn't want to be like a punch-drunk fighter, going around and reliving that big moment. At first I felt a letdown. I thought everything would be downhill from there. In time I felt sort of relieved. That feeling gradually turned into a great sense of satisfaction. Now, I could go enjoy myself, my family. For a period of two or three years I just let off. No competition, no pressure. I just enjoyed the ocean. Eventually I stopped going to the Islands. It was years before I returned.

PROLOGUE TO THE PAST

If I've learned anything in the past decade or two, it's that you never have friends like the ones you make when you're young. I thought I could take my family and go to the far ends of the earth and do whatever I wanted. I thought I could have total control of my life and decide just when I was going to do whatever I wanted to do. And I thought I wouldn't miss anybody, not even miss my ocean.

Well, I'm on the ocean now. I bang around on it in my boat. I fish. But I find I do miss just getting in the water like a duck and doing a little bodysurfing. And I do miss certain other things, like sunshine. It rains a lot here in Northern California.

And I find that I do miss some of the guys that I grew up with—guys like Dewey, Velzy, Sonny Vardeman, Bing, Bruce Brown, Mike Stange. We did a lot of trickstering, huckstering and monkeying around. Shared good times.

The guys up here in Crescent City are different. These aren't the guys I grew up with. They aren't Henry and Buffalo. My old friends wouldn't recognize me here at the harbor. I put on a different face, slow way down, spit on the ground every few words and say, "How's she doin'?" Because if you talk like you're from Southern California, people here just turn around and walk away from you. The past several years have been a real adjustment period for me, but I've adjusted.

In recent years I've also reestablished contact with some of my old friends. Mike Stange now lives only a few hours away, so we go fishing together for salmon and steelhead whenever we can. I've exposed myself to the surf industry again. I didn't realize, deep down inside, how much I missed those old guys. It's been hard for me to admit this, because I don't like to admit that I can't go somewhere and not need anybody.

Now when I go down to Southern California, what I enjoy is having a beer with guys like Hobie and Dick Metz. It's an enjoyable experience because all their success and money doesn't get in the way. We can sit and drink beer, bullshit about the old days and it's neat. One time, Metz picked me up for dinner and we drove to a restaurant in Capistrano Beach. We walked in through the bar where it was dark. As my eyes adjusted, I started to recognize all these guys—Pat Curren, Hobie, Hevs McClelland, Walter and Flippy Hoffman, Mickey Muñoz, Bob Patterson, Velzy. It was like the old days, except nowadays, we eat more than we drink.

Now and then a writer from one of the surf magazines somehow gets my number and calls me for an interview. It knocks them off their pins when I say that I'm not interested. They ask me, "Why not?" And I say, "I've left all that behind me. Besides, who really cares?"

Never in my wildest dreams did I ever think that surfing would come to what it is today, surrounded by so much bullshit. All the commercialism and the sagging bleachers with the cheering crowds. Back in the early seventies, when I closed my book on it, I thought that surfing was out of hand and had reached an intolerable point of commercialism. And now, here I am, reopening the book. Is that wise or is it better to let the past be?

Wise or not, I'd just like to tell my version of the story. My memory for dates isn't the greatest. Dates aren't that important, anyway. What is important is your recollection of people and places, your feelings. I've done the best I can to remember all the details. If I've left somebody out or screwed up on a few dates or details—well, that's the way it goes after you've spent a lifetime on the ocean. Your memory gets a little washed out. But you never forget the feeling.

Other Recollections

DUKE BOYD
Founder of Hang Ten International

Greg occupied the end of the surfing world where no one else stood. He was the epitome of the big-wave rider, with all the operatic drama behind him. With his black-and-white jailhouse trunks, he carved a

13

garish, overwhelming, showboatish figure on the biggest waves ever ridden by any man. He wanted no one else to get credit for his waves.

At two hundred and twenty-five pounds of massive muscle, Greg was like a Mack truck. Hobie Alter was more the General Motors of the surfing world. Greg was the bull the others fought.

Waimea Bay and the outside reefs are where Greg made his mark. Greg rode these in a pure way, by paddling out over a mile in some instances, surviving a wipeout and making it back to shore, all under his own power. Someday, it will be made easy. A surfer will be taken to the outer reefs in a boat. There will be oxygen tanks and a helicopter for rescue. But Greg will always be known as the man who rode the biggest, longest, most dramatic waves, while the feats of the others will fade.

GROWING UP IN
MANHATTAN BEACH

I've been stoked on the ocean since I was a kid. I got hooked on fishing when I was six, and learned to surf a few years after that at the Manhattan Beach Pier.

My mother and I had moved from San Diego to Manhattan Beach in 1943. We'd lived in San Diego since I'd been born, in 1937, the only child of Grace and Robert Lawhead. I was only three when they divorced.

In Manhattan Beach we lived about seven houses north of the Manhattan Beach Pier. Mom worked. Whenever I could I'd stay out on the pier all day and into the evening, learning about the fish, the ocean and the tides from the older fishermen. By the time I was eight, I'd got myself a job dishing bait on the pier.

A few years later my mom met and married Ash Noll, a chemical engineer with Allied Chemical. He became one the most positive influences I was ever to have on my life.

I started surfing in 1948, when I was eleven, during the summer before seventh grade. Every day, as I was walking to and from the bait house, I'd see Jack Wise, Barney Briggs, Larry Felker, Dale Velzy and all the other guys who made up the Manhattan Beach Surf Club, surfing the waves beside the pier. It looked like so much fun, I thought, "I've just gotta do that." So I cornered some guy with an old redwood surfboard and got him to sell it to me. He took my money for some old hunk of junk that he was probably going to push off some cliff for a surf sacrifice. Instead he sacrificed it to me for fifteen dollars.

It was a lot of money and a lot of board to be pushing down the street. It would take me forty-five minutes just to get the board in the water. It was made of solid redwood and weighed about a hundred and ten pounds—twenty pounds more than I weighed! I nailed some roller-skate wheels onto a wood plank and used that to push the board down to the beach. My mom would help me push it to the steps at the pier. Then I'd give the board a shove and watch it bounce down the steps. The fin would come off every time, so I left a couple of sixpenny nails at the base of the stairs near a rock that I'd use to pound the fin back on. Then I'd drag the board to the water and try to surf it.

When I was done for the day I'd leave the board under the pier, sometimes for two or three days at a time, as long as the surf looked good. If it looked like it was going bad for a while, or if I had to be someplace else for a few days, I'd get someone to help me carry the board back up the stairs and put it back on my skate plank. Then I'd push it home, seven houses the other side of the pier.

It's amazing how long it took to get to the point where you could stand up on those redwood boards and just ride a little soup. A few summers ago I built a surfboard for my two youngest kids, Ashlyne and Jed, and took them down to San Onofre. Within a half-dozen waves they were standing up. I spent my entire first summer trying to catch a wave. I'd take that board out and just stuff it into the sand and scare the sand crabs, time after time. When I finally did catch and ride a wave, I felt like I had conquered the world.

The Manhattan Beach Surf Club began as just a bunch of loose guys. When I started hanging around them, my parents thought it was a healthy thing. They had nothing else to compare it to. The only thing they would get concerned about was the outward appearance of some of these guys. They looked really scroungey.

Surfing in those days was different from what you see today. Surfers were grubby guys who spent most of their time in the water. Some worked as lifeguards. Some didn't work at all. They spoke a funny language and nobody understood them. The city fathers had given the Manhattan Beach Surf Club a little spot under the pier, hoping that they'd clean up their act and not spread themselves all over the beach. The city also gave them a bunch of rules that nobody bothered to obey.

One of these rules was that there could be no members in the club under eighteen. I guess the city figured that these guys would be a bad influence on minors. It's true, they were an influence on this minor and on my friend and surfing accomplice Bing Copeland, but I doubt that either of us would have called their influence "bad."

Bing Copeland started surfing that same summer that I did. There was another kid, Buzzy Bent, who surfed at his home turf of Windansea. I first met Buzzy at the annual luau that was held at Windansea. I had hitched a ride down there with a couple of the guys from the Manhattan Beach Surf Club. Buzzy and I became buddies, and I ended up spending two weeks with him, surfing Windansea every day. He was a year older than me and Bing. Years later, after Bing and I had become established surfboard manufacturers, Buzzy teamed up with Hawaiian surfing champion Joey Cabell to form The Chart House restaurant chain. But, in 1948, the three of us were the only young kids surfing in Southern California.

Since Bing and I hung around the club so much of the time and eventually learned to surf pretty well, the guys in the club made us honorary members. They called Bing and me their Everlasting Mascots and wrote in the club's bylaws that there could be no other kids but us. Bing and I were honored. We went to all the meetings and hung out with these guys for several years. We grew up quickly, surrounded by guys eighteen and older, in their prime. They lived to surf, drink, raise hell and score heavily with women. I saw these guys going up and down the coast on surf trips, drinking and bagging girls, and all I could think of was "What a neat life!"

I'll never forget that first summer. One time, after surfing Windansea, Larry Felker and a couple of the guys took Bing and me down to Tijuana and indoctrinated us into the world of wine and women. I was a pretty skinny little guy at age eleven. This big ol' gal reached down and grabbed me by the hand, almost jerked me off the floor. She bellowed out, "Ya got four dollars, sonny? If ya do, come with me!" It was scarier than twenty-foot Waimea.

After a summer of being hauled up and down the coast from Malibu to Windansea by assorted characters from the Manhattan Beach Surf Club, starting seventh grade was quite an adjustment. I no longer had much in common with other kids my age. They were playing silly games, pulling girls' pigtails. All the while I'm wondering, "Where are the wine and women?"

Bing and I used to save our school lunch money and get one of the guys to buy us a jug of wine. We'd take it down to the clubhouse at the pier. You grew up in a hurry when your mentors were guys like Dale Velzy, Larry Felker and Barney Briggs.

The next summer, stories started filtering down to us about some guy named Ricky Grigg, who was doing squatting island pull-outs at Malibu. Ricky's sister, Robin, had gotten him interested in surfing. Charlie Reimers and Mickey Muñoz came on the scene a year or so after Ricky. About this same time, Gard Chapin had started taking his stepson, Mickey Dora, to San Onofre, and Phil Edwards was making his mark as The Guayule Kid, so-called after a spot he regularly surfed a couple miles below Carlsbad. The first board that Phil Edwards ever bought was my third board, a balsa board that had Sylvester the Cat painted on the nose. I bought that board new from Joe Quigg, used it for a summer, then sold it to Bev Morgan. He surfed it for two years, then sold it to Phil. All these guys became great surfers in their own right.

One day I took off to Malibu with some of the guys from the Manhattan Beach Surf Club. I never told my folks where I was going. When I rolled in about nine o'clock that night, I had to stand in front of the firing squad and explain why, at age eleven, I thought I could get in a car with a bunch of older guys and go thirty miles up the coast without telling anyone. My folks had been all over the pier, looking for me. When I told them where I had been, they calmed down a little. My mom was pretty outgoing. She had been down to the pier to meet Velzy and the gang. I guess they had given her the impression of being like big brothers to me. A real snow job! We had a big talk about my going off to Malibu without telling them. "You've got to tell us these things, Son," they said. From then on I did, but I think my folks already knew that they had lost control of me—it had happened the first time I pushed that redwood board down to the pier.

During eighth grade I used to go down to the pier in the mornings to surf before school. I'd wake up Bev Morgan at the Manhattan Beach Surf Club, and he'd go with me. Morgan was already out of high school and drove this cut, chopped and lowered black Chevy with chrome pipes and a hole in the back window where the surfboards could stick out. That Chevy was quite a showpiece and any kid's dream car.

Morgan and I had a deal. In exchange for a big, hot breakfast at my house after surfing, he'd drive me to school. We timed it to perfection. When all the kids were lined up, waiting to go into class, we'd roll up in the Chevy, revving the motor—rummmm, rummmm, rummmm. Morgan would get out, open my door and dust me off with a whisk broom, as though he were my personal chauffeur. All my buddies and teachers were there, watching our routine. I loved seeing their reactions.

Morgan eventually started a shop called Dive 'n Surf in Hermosa Beach. He later sold it to Bill and Bob Meistrell, who soon afterward started the Body Glove wetsuit line. Morgan is now retired and lives part of the year at The Ranch, a well-known surf spot near Santa Barbara. The Meistrells and their sons still run Dive 'n Surf and Body Glove International.

Other Recollections

MIKE DOYLE
1969 World Surfing Champion

I grew up in Westchester, by the L.A. International Airport. In those days that was considered real inland. No one surfed at my school but me.

I first became aware of surfing in 1956, at age twelve. Up until then, I skimboarded and even rode shorebreak waves on the same skimboard. Early one morning at the Manhattan Beach Pier, when the surf was four to five feet I saw all these guys out riding waves—I couldn't believe it. That was when I started getting stoked on surfing. I went every day to watch and to retrieve lost boards so I could get in a quick paddle before one of the surfers swam in for his board. Just touching these surfboards gave me a thrill. I had bruises all over me from these lost boards hitting me, and I couldn't care less.

Later I became aware of who these guys were and their riding styles—Dale Velzy, Greg Noll, Bob Hogan, George Kapu. Velzy was shaping and glassing boards under the pier. I became an avid watcher, to say the least. I remember looking in each of their cars in the parking lot. One day I saw a big shiny trophy in Bob Hogan's '41 Ford. On that same day, I saw Greg Noll turn around and ride a wave backwards. Shit! I thought I'd die with excitement.

Greg was skinny then, around nineteen, I'd guess. About five years younger than the rest of the guys. He was hot. You could sense it just watching him.

I talked my mom into buying my first board then, a nine-foot, six-inch Velzy and Jacobs balsa board with thirty-two ants in the glass job.

Velzy told me the ants wouldn't hurt anything and I believed him. I remember my mom's words: "This board is probably just like everything else you want. You'll use it for a week and throw it away."

I showed her! We still laugh about it. Mom painted a totem pole on that first board and later I sold it to the real Gidget for fifteen bucks. At the time, my father was in the Navy at Point Mugu. He drove past Malibu every day—a great deal for me! I became "Malibu Mike" and was at Malibu during the sixties, during the renaissance era of surfing, when Mickey Dora, Gidget, the Beach Boys and all the excitement of surfing was coming on strong. In those days, when the Big South started pumping, every hot surfer on the coast would come to Malibu, the true proving grounds.

Other Recollections

RICKY GRIGG
Surfer, Professor of Oceanography and Marine Ecology

I got into surfing because I was there and it was happening around me. My sister liked Tommy Zahn. He lifeguarded at Malibu and got her interested in surfing. She became the hottest gal on the whole coast.

Buzzy Trent was my hero. I used to sit at his lifeguard station and listen to him tell stories. He took me surfing when I was nine years old. My sister was out there with us. It was like the beginning of a whole subculture. Hearing about the other surfers in these little pockets up and down the coast, we almost became mythological to each other. Then we started traveling and meeting at different spots and it was great. We built on each other's experience.

When I was eleven I got hurt pretty badly while surfing at State Beach. On a wipeout, my board whipped up under my ribs real hard and busted my spleen in half. Buzzy Trent was ten or fifteen yards ahead of me in a sand-buster and he got me to the beach. For three or four minutes, I couldn't get any air. Buzzy was doing what he could and, finally, I started breathing again. Then Buzzy took me to the hospital in his '39 Packard.

I think Dewey Weber may have come closer than anyone during that time to falling right on the edge of the "Max Headroom" style that you see among young surfers today. But I can remember a time when no one turned faster than Greg Noll. He took on a different style when he ran into big waves. That's when he got the name Da Bull. He'd sit out there like an immovable object. But when he was fourteen or fifteen years old, he was the best hotdogger on the California Coast. He could whip a board back and forth before Dewey Weber had ever heard of surfing.

There's something really magnetic about the ocean. I think if I live to be eighty, I'll never forget some of my first times surfing, where the first glimpse that I got of the ocean each day would be reflected in my attitude for the rest of the day. Whether there was surf. Whether there wasn't surf. And even if there was no surf and the ocean was dead calm, if the wind was blowing just a little bit offshore. . . . Pretty conditions like that made you feel really good inside and you'd go skipping along your way. And if it was all grunchy and the wind was blowing on shore and making whitecaps—well, that also was reflected in your attitude. Everything would be kind of grunchy that day.

I find it really hard now to go back to Southern California. I go down there every year to keep my lifeguard certification current with Los Angeles County. They require three days on the beach and a little swim. One time, they assigned me to a spot next to the jetty in Santa Monica. Block after block are all these million-dollar homes, surrounded by huge wrought-iron fences and locked gates. I was riding in the lifeguard truck with my old friend Wally Millican, and I asked him what these big fences were all about. He said, "Well, when the sun goes down, this place just buttons up."

He pointed out an area where some guy was shotgunned to death just three days before, right there on the Strand. The blood was still on the pavement. They had had something like six murders along the Strand within that last year. I got to thinking, who in hell would spend a million bucks to come live in a place like this?

Where I now live, in Crescent City, you can go out and walk a mile down the beach by yourself, drive down the beach, collect driftwood if you want. The dilemma is, Southern California has the neatest weather and the neatest surf spots for kids growing up. I hate to see my kids miss that.

MIKE STANGE
Surfer, Retired Los Angeles County Lifeguard

In 1947 my older brother, Pete, became one of the very first county beach lifeguards, so I grew up around the water and around some real characters. Fred Beckner, a city lifeguard, used to take me and my neighbor Don out into the old channel at Playa del Rey in the middle of winter on rubber surf mats when the surf was huge. We'd go out beyond the jaws of the two jetties and pick up waves that must have been twelve feet high. I remember I could see the beaches on both sides of the jetties, Venice and Del Rey, when I was on top of the wave, ready to speed down its face. I could hear Beckner, laughing and shouting at us, "O.K., O.K., ha ha, paddle, paddle, take off!" Don and I were about ten. The old-timers didn't have much pity.

In those days the lifeguards used hollow boards made by an early redwood-board surfer, Pete Peterson. We called them kook boxes because you felt like a kook on them. I remember riding one of them at Playa del Rey. You'd stand up way on the back to turn the thing. There was no way you could really maneuver it like a surfboard.

I started surfing at El Porto, about a year after Greg started at Manhattan Beach. I was going to El Segundo High and very few people surfed El Porto. Of course, I knew of Greg, because the surfers at the Manhattan Beach Pier were the main group, the innovators of everything.

In 1953, at one of Bud Browne's surfing movies in the Santa Monica Auditorium, Greg came up and asked me if I was going to the Islands that next winter. I was surprised that he was so friendly. We, the 42nd Street Surfers, were kind of low-key and low on the totem pole in the surfing world, and considered by most people to be kooks. Greg and I became friends. That same year, we both lied about our age and took the lifeguard test together. We passed, and started working on the beach. That was when I became more known in the surf community.

When I first moved up to Crescent City, I tried surfing in a wetsuit

22

for the first time. The water is much colder up there than it is off the southern part of the coast. You sometimes see surfers in full wetsuits, from hood to booties. But I couldn't stand having all that rubber on me, or having something between the bottom of my feet and the board.

From the time I started surfing at age eleven until I was thirty-five, I think I was in the water more than I was out of it. I think my body got to the point where it could actually withstand cold temperatures. When wetsuits became popular and were being worn practically year-round in Southern California, I still didn't wear them. Guys couldn't believe that I'd be out there on a cold winter day wearing only my trunks.

Southern California is blessed with some really nice surf conditions. In Northern California, we get some good surf, but we often end up with a lot of storms right on top of us because we're closer to the source. Down South the storm centers are generally far enough away to where the swells have traveled two thousand to three thousand miles from the Aleutians and are cleaned up by the time they hit shore.

The one place I regret not having surfed on the South Coast is Redondo before the breakwater was built. The older guys would tell us, "You'll drown if you go out there, kid." But I remember watching some absolutely perfect waves. Some of that stuff was eighteen to twenty foot and was just cream puff stuff compared to the Islands. But there was a seawall then, and if you lost your board, it was a goner. Before the breakwater was built, the high tide would come in and crash into the houses. It would have been a dangerous place for a kid just starting out, but it could have been done.

Other Recollections

SONNY VARDEMAN
Lieutenant, Los Angeles County Dept. of Beaches and Harbors

One day, during the winter of 1960, the surf broke about twenty feet at the Redondo breakwater. Greg and I and a few of our friends had been out riding a few big waves the previous day. In fact, one of our rides appeared in an early issue of *Surfer* magazine. The following day, the swell was huge. We couldn't get off the beach, so everybody backed out.

23

Everybody, that is, but Greg. He went out inside the breakwater where the boats were moored, then paddled out and around the jetty to get to the break.

On the way out around the jetty, a giant set came and almost caught Greg between it and the seawall. He just made it over the top of the wave. Had it broken, it would have slammed him into the seawall. The set was so big, it rolled over the seawall and tore a number of boats lose from their moorings. It had to be twenty feet. He finally made it to where the peak was breaking. After about forty-five minutes, another giant set came. He paddled for one of the bigger ones, caught it and rode it half a mile back to the beach as we all watched from shore. Greg had put himself in a very precarious position along the breakwater jetty. But he was very determined to ride the wave, come hell or high water. When he was that determined, he usually accomplished whatever it was he'd set out to do.

VELZY

Velzy's a classic. Absolutely an incredible person. What I like about him is that he's never changed. He's still shaping boards at his house. Last time I saw him, he was hand-shaping hot curl redwood boards—wallhangers. He told me that each one takes about a month to make. He was selling them for a thousand bucks apiece to rich guys—doctors, lawyers, dentists. Some of them surf, but not on these hot curl boards.

When they ask him why the boards cost so much, Velzy says, "Damn it, you can afford it. How many teeth do you have to pull to make a thousand dollars?" Velzy is still a fifties hustler. Never try to out-hustle him. You'll lose.

The beauty of these boards is incredible. He puts about six coats of resin on them and hand rubs it out. There is no one doing anything as beautiful today as Velzy is doing with these boards. Guys who shape foam boards today, who never had any experience on redwood, would go nuts if they had to lay a power planer on one of those redwoods.

Other Recollections

DALE VELZY

One of the first surfboards I ever used belonged to someone I didn't even know. I found it sitting along the side of someone's house on 6th Street in Hermosa Beach. I used it every day one summer, until my dad, who was a lifeguard at Hermosa, agreed to help me make my own board.

We lived next door to Hoppy Swarts and Leroy Grannis, two surfers from the thirties. My dad made my first board off the design of their boards. I was eight or nine at the time. Not long after he'd made it, I ran into the pier on it and split it down the center. In those days, this would happen quite a bit. We'd just glue it back together, bolt it and put a cork in over the bolt. After you broke these boards a few times, they got a little waterlogged, so you'd have to bring them in and reshape them. That's what got me started shaping and designing boards. I became real interested in design, in making the boards work better, according to a person's weight and style.

Eventually, other guys started asking me to make changes to their boards. We didn't have fiberglass then. We didn't even varnish the boards. We'd get splinters, but we'd just take them out and keep surfing. It was a while before my dad would loan me his good tools to try my hand at shaping balsa wood. My best board was the second redwood I made for myself. I was in the Merchant Marines, and went off to the war in '44. I left my board with a friend, Ed Edgar, and told him that he was the only person who could ride it while I was gone. I came home to find out that someone had stolen the board.

It took a lot of finesse to ride those old redwoods. They were like old Cadillacs on a freeway—a real smooth ride, and everyone got out of your way.

———————

There are some real good stories about Dale Velzy. Like most South Bay surfers, he also worked for the lifeguard service. He had the night shift. He was supposed to check all the towers, from El Porto to Hermosa Beach, to make sure there was no vandalism. Half the time he'd crawl in one of the towers and sleep through his shift.

One day, a body floated up off of the Manhattan Pier. The 'guards had to go out and get it. It had been dead about a week. They put the body in one of those body baskets and wrapped a bunch of towels around it. When they got the guy into shore and the coroner's office took over, they just threw the towels in the back of a tower, intending to take care of them later.

So here comes Velzy on the night shift, looking for a place to crap out. Parks his truck, unlocks the tower door and dives into this inviting-looking pile of towels. I guess he didn't smell the rotten skin until it was too late. Legend has it that Velzy was still in the showers at Hermosa three days later, scrubbing with a wire brush.

Another time, Velzy had just finished making a racing board, a twenty-foot-long Catalina-type paddleboard. One of the biggest problems with this type of board was that they tended to broach. Velzy had devised a tiller that you could push from one side to the other with your foot. The post ran up through the board. He had worked on it for three weeks and was really proud of the thing.

One hot Sunday afternoon, I helped him carry the board down the steps at the Manhattan Beach Pier. He had decided to take it out for a little test-paddle. He paddled out without a problem. When he took off on a wave and the board began nosing down the wave, or pearling, he instinctively grabbed the rails and slid back on the board to keep the nose from going under.

The tiller went right up between his legs, got him right in the scrotum. I was watching from the beach when it happened. It really was funny, but kind of horrifying at the same time. Here comes Velzy, limping up the beach with his nuts in his hand and blood running down his legs. A lady saw him and threw up, right on the sand. I tried to help him. All he could say was, "Got me right in the sack. My jewels fell out."

Velzy was the best surfer in that time period when Bing and I were growing up. We looked up to him. I was pretty scrawny then and Velzy called me Mouse. I went everywhere with him, even up the coast to Malibu. I was his gremmie.

Velzy is mostly remembered as a great surfboard shaper, but he was a hell of a surfer, too. He had a beautiful, easy style. His whole life was geared towards surfing and getting laid. "Catch waves, drink beer and get laid as often and as many times as you possibly can," was the motto of the day. This was the influence that guys like Bing and I grew up around. How were we poor little guys supposed to turn out?

The long boardshorts that surfers wear today probably came out of a contest that Velzy, Barney Briggs and a couple of other guys decided to hold. They'd go to the Salvation Army shop, buy white sailor pants and cut them off just below the knees. They lived in these pants. By nature, anyone living the kind of bohemian lifestyle that Velzy and the others did would be pretty scroungy and dirty. Being in the water so much, they actually stayed pretty clean.

The rule governing this contest was that you had to live in these cutoffs day after day, surfing, dating, whatever. You could only unzip them in the presence of your girlfriend or to go to the bathroom. Then the pants could come down to your knees. Otherwise, they had to stay on your body. I think the contest went on for about a month before Barney gave up and Velzy was finally declared the winner.

When we first went to the Islands, these pants were kind of a trendy deal. You see us wearing them in a lot of the old pictures. Eventually, we started going to M. Nii's in Waianae and having white shorts made with stripes down the side and a pocket for our board wax. That was a big deal, to go to Hawaii and have M. Nii make your surftrunks. They caught on everywhere we went and were prized on the Mainland. We'd bring M. Nii's trunks back to our friends.

In the early sixties, Dave Rochlen started the Jams trend. Jams were—and still are—brightly colored, Hawaiian-print trunks, cut just above the knee. Every surfer wore them. Rochlen's company, Surf Line Hawaii, originally started out as a surf shop in Honolulu that was owned by Dick Metz. Now it's a big international clothing company. The original Surf Line Jams came on strong again a few years ago with the surfing crowd. But the first surfwear trend started with the cutoff sailor pants worn by Velzy and his cohorts at the Manhattan Beach Surf Club.

In the summertime, about 12 of us guys would sleep in front of the Manhattan Beach Surf Club. During the day, there were so few people around that we could just leave our sleeping bags right there in the open. One day, Bing, Bev Morgan and I were surfing at the Palos Verdes Cove and we found a dead skunk that someone had recently run over. We threw a line around its leg and dragged it back to the pier behind the car—and we put it in Velzy's sleeping bag.

Now, Velzy was a notorious womanizer. Out late every night. That particular night, we all bunked down in our sleeping bags and waited for Velzy to roll in. We had pushed his bag out a ways from ours. The smell coming from it was horrible. About two in the morning, here comes Velzy after a hot date, just drunk enough not to realize what was going on. He crawls into his sleeping bag with the dead skunk . . . suffice it to say, it was a classic prank. To this day, he has never known who did it. Now I've blown the whistle on myself.

A big, lumbering guy named Billy Barr fiberglassed boards for Velzy at the time. Barr was massive and hairy and had all sorts of trouble with the terrific itch you can get from fiberglass dust—especially when it works its way under your waistbelt and into your pants. Barr hit upon the idea of wrapping two-inch adhesive tape around his waist to prevent the dust from getting in his pants. Before he started glassing, he'd tape himself up. The worst part was taking off the tape. He'd let out a roar as he ripped it—and a big chunk of hair—off his waist. He went through this routine every day for about a week. By the end of the week, his waist was nearly hairless, but he was itch-free. Unfortunately, the bill for adhesive tape had exceeded his salary that week, and Barr decided to find a new line of work.

Barr met an unfortunate demise. Like the rest of the guys at the Manhattan Beach Surf Club, Barr enjoyed the ladies. One day, Barr got caught in an amorous position with the wife of a policeman. The guy walked in on them and emptied his gun in Barr's chest. The policeman turned himself in and served a few years. But Billy was gone forever.

Everything went really well between Velzy and me for about three years. He built boards at the Manhattan Pier and I hung around all the time, soaking up all I could about shaping balsa-wood boards. One day, Velzy and Billy Barr decided to go to lunch together. He'd been working on a board and I asked him if I could just take off the rough wood with a drawknife while he was gone. Velzy said, "Yeah, but don't do any more than that or you'll screw up the board."

Velzy and Barr ended up in some saloon until late afternoon. Rolled in shit-faced about four o'clock. By that time, I had finished shaping the whole board. Velzy walked in, picked up the board, looked down the deck. Looked over at me. Looked down one rail, looked over at me. Looked down the other rail, looked over at me. Looked at the bottom . . . That was the last board I ever shaped for Velzy. Time to wean the gremmie.

Two months later, I was doing reshapes, and not long after that, I was shaping new boards under my own name. Velzy and I remained good friends all through the years, but I wasn't his little gremmie any more. I was the competition.

There weren't that many people on the coast then who could shape balsa wood. Besides Velzy, there were Bob Simmons, Joe Quigg, Matt Kivlin, Dave Rochlen and Hobie Alter. Hobie was just getting under way at that time. Rochlen, Kivlin and Quigg were the Malibu gang. Their

"Malibu boards" were more maneuverable than anything around and revolutionized board design during that time.

Most of these boards came out of garage operations. Kivlin was getting into architecture and Quigg was becoming interested in catamarans. Rochlen was on his way to Hawaii and the introduction of Surf Line Jams. Velzy was really the first that I know of to have a full-on, full-time surf shop.

Velzy has been from the outhouse to the penthouse. He's a living museum piece. He's still shaping boards on special order and he's enjoying himself. He's got his niche in life and he seems satisfied with what he's doing. Some guys get to a certain point, a certain age and reach a peaceful thing. I think Velzy is there. The guy is still my hero.

GONE SURFING

Through most of high school, I was gone surfing anytime I could get a ride with the guys I knew from Redondo High. When we were freshmen at Mira Costa High, Bing and I were the only guys who surfed. As soon as school let out, our buddies from Redondo High would be there with their cars and boards, waiting to pick us up. The guys at our school wondered, "What is this surfing deal?"

By the time we were sophomores, in '52, guys like Mike Bright, Sonny Vardeman and Steve Voorhees had come into the surf scene and we started seeing more and more younger guys get interested. The school officials were concerned about the surfing craze. Some of the guys who normally would have been going out for sports were surfing instead. They didn't care about the letter on the sweater and the squealing girls in the grandstands. I shared their feelings.

During one of my many trips to the principal's office, I was asked, "What do you guys do down there at the Manhattan Beach Surf Club? What are your goals, what do you want to become?" I told him that I wanted to surf, I wanted to make surfboards, I wanted to go to Hawaii, I wanted to see the world and have a good time. From the principal's point of view, that qualified me as most likely to end up a beach bum and never amount to shit.

I learned about shaping balsa wood by watching Velzy at his shop, by the Manhattan Beach Pier. Later, when I was fourteen, I teamed up with Mike Bright. He was from Hermosa Beach. We called him Bones because of his bony physique. Bones was a hell of an athlete. He won a lot of paddleboard races, including the Catalina and Diamond Head races, and went on to become an All-American volleyball player. Bones also was one of the first professional beach volleyball players. Later, he owned a dive shop in Malibu for a while. Unfortunately, his athletic days came to an end one day when he was out diving and got bent. He ended up in a wheelchair.

But, in our early years, Bones and I got a little business going, reshaping balsa boards. Bones had, or thought he had, a little experience in glassing boards. Just like I thought I had experience in shaping them. Guys who were unhappy with their boards would bring them to us. We'd strip them down, I'd reshape them and Mike would fiberglass them. We made some real beauties.

Except for one particular board. We set it up in Bones' backyard on a couple of sawhorses. We stripped it down and reshaped it, then Bones started laying on the fiberglass and resin. He accidentally kicked the sawhorse leg and the board fell off into the sand. He tried to brush the sand off, but, of course, it was stuck in the resin. Finally, Bones just stood up and said, "Well, you won't ever have to wax this board. It has built-in traction."

The type of fiberglass first used on surfboards required sun-curing. The catalyst then used was activated by the sun. You'd get weird results, like only half the board would set up. You'd finish glassing a board and the sun would go behind a cloud, slimming your chances of getting an even cure. We had to work with stuff like this for a couple of years before any advancements in fiberglass, resins or catalysts occurred.

When I was about fifteen, my folks moved from our house on the Strand to a big adobe house a little farther away. My bedroom was big and became a great place to store balsa wood.

One time, I knew that a shipment was due in at General Veneer from South America, so I made sure that I got there early. I spent a day and a half going through the shipment, looking for all the best wood. I creamed the place, got all the lightest wood, a thousand board-feet in all. The only balsa that was left at General Veneer after I finished was either ruined with rot, too heavy or screwed up in some way.

I stored all of the wood in my bedroom, leaving one little trail to my bed. My folks had bought me an old Maul planer for my birthday that must have weighed about fifty pounds. I shaped the boards in my backyard.

One day, I got a call from another surfboard shaper, Bob "Ole" Olson: "You dirty bastard, you cleaned out General Veneer!" A friend of his, Bruce Brown, had asked Olson to make him a board, but Olson couldn't find any good balsa. He asked me, "How about selling me enough to make a board for a buddy of mine?"

I agreed, and they came over that day. Olson and I negotiated over the price as Bruce listened in. He never said a word. He was eating a can of tuna, using the bent lid as a spoon. I was watching him out of the corner of my eye. He took a shot at a big bite, missed it and it fell on the floor. He nonchalantly kicked it under my bed. I said, "Hey, man, this is my bedroom." I mean, the crummy guy just kicked a pile of dead fish under my bed and he wants to negotiate for some of my prime balsa wood?

Over the years, Bruce and I became great pals. I never missed an opportunity to remind Bruce of the circumstances surrounding our first meeting. As it turned out, we traveled to Mazatlán together, shared a house on the North Shore of Oahu, and we both made surf films. Bruce's claim to fame is the all-time classic surf movie, *The Endless Summer.*

Other Recollections

SONNY VARDEMAN

Greg and I have been friends since grade school. While he belonged to the Manhattan Beach Surf Club, I was a member of a surf club called the Hermosa Beach Seals, along with our friends Mike Bright and Steve Voorhees. We'd see each other at the beach all the time. During the early fifties, there were very few surfers. You'd see the same guys at the different spots up and down the coast. That's how we all got to know each other.

In high school, we all hung out on the beach together. Mike Bright and a few of us played on the football and basketball teams, then surfed during the summer. Greg wasn't much into high school athletics. He hung out at the Manhattan Beach Surf Club, spent most of his time on the beach. Greg is a very proud man. He doesn't like to be a loser. I think that's what made him good in paddleboard racing. I also think that was one of the reasons he didn't go out for high school athletics. If Greg can't do something well, he won't participate in it.

Greg devoted most of his energy to surfing. Buzzy Trent, Joe

Quigg, Dale Velzy, Bob Simmons and George Downing were all six or seven years older than we were. They're the guys we watched. George lived in Hawaii, but came to the Mainland for paddleboard races. Buzzy was a lifeguard around Santa Monica and Malibu. He went over to the Islands in the early fifties and became one of the pioneers of modern surfing at Makaha and of big-wave surfing. Greg really learned about big-wave riding from Buzzy. If you compare films of Buzzy and Greg, you can see that Greg emulated Buzzy's style. Greg admired George Downing, but he emulated Buzzy's style.

Greg was always pretty much a daredevilish guy. During our senior year, Greg, Steve Voorhees and a couple of other guys took part of the year off and went to Hawaii to high school. This was a big move in those days for a seventeen-year-old guy. Greg would have gone with or without his parents' blessings, but, luckily, Greg had a tremendous amount of respect for his stepfather, Ash Noll, and they communicated quite well. Greg explained to Ash that it meant a lot to him to be able to make the move to Hawaii to surf and go to school. I'm sure Ash said, "If it means that much to you, then do it." From that point on, Greg was stuck on surfing and on Hawaii.

In 1955, when we graduated from high school, we were finally old enough to be lifeguards, and several of us took the test together. Greg had lied about his age a couple of years before and got in ahead of us. This was during the Korean conflict, and the government was drafting heavily out of our senior class. Greg joined the Coast Guard Reserves. Meanwhile, I took my first trip to the Islands that October, with Steve Voorhees, Bing Copeland, Mike Bright and Rick Stoner. To avoid the draft, Voorhees and I joined the navy at Pearl Harbor. Copeland and Stoner went into active duty in the Coast Guard.

After a service break of a couple of years, some of us came back and went to college. Greg continued with the lifeguards and making surf-boards out of his garage. Greg was a pretty curious guy. He'd learned a lot from watching Velzy and Bob Simmons. He was constantly on Velzy's tail, watching his every move. This is how he learned about shaping balsa-wood boards.

Greg built me a couple of balsa boards. There was such a demand for surfboards then that you'd have to look someone up and beg them to build one. Materials were hard to get, even if you knew where to get them. The labor and skill involved in building a board wasn't easy.

Bing Copeland, Rick Stoner, Mike Bright and I started messing with surfboards, too, in my folks' big, two-car garage in Hermosa Beach. Bing and Rick shaped while Mike and I glassed. It was a bad scene. We had sawhorses lined up and down the alley, and my dad was getting mad as hell. He finally kicked us out, saying, "You guys are running a commercial enterprise down here. If you're going to be in business, find yourselves a shop." This is how Bing's and Rick's shop on the Strand evolved. They became partners.

By that time, Greg had outgrown his garage operation and had gone up on Coast Highway in Manhattan Beach and opened a shop in 1956, after he and Beverly had gotten married. They were in Manhattan Beach for a brief time, then they set up shop in Hermosa, on Pier Avenue and Coast Highway.

I started a fiberglassing shop with Mike Bright, called Surf Fiberglass. We specialized in fiberglassing and did work for several surfboard makers, including Greg, Dewey Weber and Hap Jacobs. As their businesses expanded, they eventually started doing their own glassing. In the sixties, I jumped in with my own surfboard shop in Huntington Beach. Throughout the sixties, Huntington Beach was hot. The sixties were surfing's boom days.

Part of the reason for the boom was that surfing had caught on on the East Coast. Greg, Hobie and Dewey did promotional tours on the East Coast and came back with hundreds of orders for surfboards. During that time, each of their shops was turning out hundreds of boards a week.

Then it began to slow down. After shipping thousands of boards to their Eastern accounts, the East Coast shops got a little careless with their accounts. Some of them started making their own boards. In the latter part of the sixties, East Coast business turned sour. At the same time, the Vietnam War was escalating and all the young men went off to war. There was a general downturn in the surf business. A lot of the board manufacturers on the West Coast were severely hurt. Jacobs and Bing sold out. Greg hung on for a while and eventually dissolved in the early seventies. By that time, I also had closed up shop and gone back to lifeguarding full time.

35

During high school, I met my wife, Beverly. We both were sophomores. I was the high school letch and she was a beach gal, a very good-looking gal, and I was really attracted to her. She had, and still has, a really strong personality. Beverly and I went through all the stages of the surf thing together. She became the motivational force behind the whole surfboard operation, kept all the pieces in place as the business grew and expanded.

We got married almost a year after high school, a few months after I got back from competing in the paddling championships in Australia. We lived in a little house on Homer Street in Manhattan Beach. During the summer, I worked as a lifeguard at the Manhattan Beach Pier, for about a dollar forty-four an hour. At the time, those were good part-time wages.

As soon as I got home from working as a lifeguard, I'd go back to work in my garage, shaping new boards. I was grinding out about ten boards a week from this little two-car garage. I had an automatic router machine, the whole deal. This was the late fifties, and surfing was starting to get very popular. I outgrew the garage operation within a year or so.

We rented a small shop on the highway in Manhattan Beach and moved the business there until we outgrew that space. Found another place in Hermosa Beach across from a school and stayed there for about five years. We were so busy that we'd be making surfboards out in front of the shop, almost overflowing into the street. Surfers would hang out, watching us work. One day, the building inspector came by while we were outside, gluing up boards on sawhorses. He just shook his head. We were causing too much of a commotion, he told us, and causing traffic snarls.

That and the fact that surfing had caught fire on the East Coast prompted us to build our twenty-thousand-square-foot surfboard factory and shop on Valley Drive in Hermosa. It opened in October of '65 and became the permanent home for Greg Noll Surfboards until we closed up shop in '71.

Other Recollections

BEVERLY

I was a goody two-shoes in high school. I didn't stay out after ten. I was a good little girl. A cheerleader, involved in all sorts of school activities. Greg was involved in absolutely nothing but surfing.

Greg was pretty much a man of the world at age fifteen. He and Bing Copeland used to come to football games. Here I am, cheering for the home team, and I'd see Greg and Bing, arriving late in the game. They'd sit up in the bleachers. Greg always wore this awful Salvation Army trenchcoat. He liked it because he could stow a gallon of wine under it. Here he is to take me home and I am mortified, but I would go.

He just confused me. I couldn't understand at first why he confused me so. Every time he would get around me, I became flustered. I've known this man for thirty-five, forty, a hundred thousand years, it seems, and to this day, he still flusters me.

I chose the Coast Guard Reserves for my time in the service. In California, the commitment at that time was a few weeks' active duty a year, plus monthly meetings.

Hawaii was not yet a state, but the Coast Guard had a base there. Since I was spending so much time in the Islands, I would transfer part of my time in service over there. I'd contact my local Reserve Office before I left for the Islands, then, when I'd arrive in Hawaii, I'd contact the Reserve Office there after I was well into my two- or three-month stay, then put in a meeting or two before heading back to the Mainland. I wouldn't tell the Reserve Office on the Mainland that I was back until a month or two before I got ready to go to the Islands again. Then I'd do a little active reserve duty, go to a meeting and split.

The whole thing worked out to where in four years I was honorably discharged after having completed maybe four weeks' total active reserve duty and having attended about half the meetings I was supposed to. They can't retain you in any one area, and they were never really sure where I was. It was a perfect deal for me.

I couldn't resist pulling a few pranks, even in the service. During one tour of active reserve duty, we were under the thumb of a couple of asshole petty officers who didn't like us any more than we liked them. On the day of a big parade, another guy and I managed to put some chopped fiberglass in these officers' jockstraps. There's nothing that irritates your skin more than fiberglass. During the parade, these guys looked like bowlegged cowboys. They suspected that my buddy and I had done it, but they weren't able to prove it. You might say that the war between us and the officers escalated after that prank.

But my buddies and I had the last word on those jerks. At the end of an active reserve tour, the commandant leads a giant final inspection. We got one of those guys good. Right before inspection, we put a turd on a paper towel and placed it underneath the blanket over his pillow. We messed up the bed a little, to be sure to draw attention to it. Of course, as he came marching through the barracks, the commandant spotted the messy bed. His assistant ripped off the bedcovers and the turd fell out, right on the commandant's foot. We're talking about the head honcho, with poop on his shoe.

I'm sure we'd have been court-martialed if they had caught us. There were only three of us in on the prank, but the officers grilled every one of the hundred and fifty guys in the company, one at a time. Nobody cracked. At the end of the day, as we were leaving through the gate, one of the officers said to me, "Noll, I know goddamn well that you did it. I can't prove it, but I know it was you." I said, "Well, that's the way it goes, sir," and gave him a snappy salute.

HIGH SCHOOL,
HAWAIIAN-STYLE

The first time I went to Hawaii was in the fall of '54. We'd all heard about older guys like Buzzy Trent, Flippy and Walter Hoffman living in quonset huts at Makaha. I couldn't wait to go. I was seventeen, six or seven years younger than these guys and still in high school. To live and go to school in Hawaii, I'd need a guardian. I found one in Billy Ming, a surfer about seven years older. Somehow I bullshitted my folks into believing that Billy Ming was a fine, upstanding individual and that he was going to be my guardian while I finished high school in the Islands.

Other Recollections

BEVERLY

Greg always has done just as he pleases. I don't think it was a matter of his parents giving up on him. When Greg told his parents that he wanted to go to high school in Hawaii, I think his father, Ash, understood that Greg needed to have his freedom. Otherwise, he knew, there would be problems.

Greg's determination and dominating strength come from his mother. They're very much alike. The same hold she has on him, he has on other people. As a young man, Greg lived and breathed surfing. There was nothing else as important to him. He made it very clear to me that if I could fit into that scheme and go along with him, that was fine. If not, I would be history. I never even considered not doing what Greg wanted to do. I was in awe of him and would have followed him off the edge of the world.

We went together through high school. When Greg went away to school in the Islands, I'd date a little, but it was more like pals dating pals. All of my friends and Greg's friends grew up together. We were together on the beach all the time. I always hung out around the guys—Sonny, Bones, Steve Voorhees. We were the 17th Street Group, and Greg was from the Manhattan Beach Pier Group. The guys stole each other's waves, we had water-balloon and rotten-egg fights, all the things kids do. When Greg and I got together, it was a natural thing for us to still do everything with all these guys. I was often the only woman along.

Steve Voorhees, Mike Stange, Billy Ming and a couple of other guys we knew also went with me that winter. We found a big quonset hut to live in at Makaha. I had bought an old truck to drive back and forth between Makaha and school. Whenever the surf was up, Ming wrote me any kind of excuse I needed to stay home and surf.

The nearest high school was Waipahu High. There were two haoles in the whole school, myself and a girl. The rest were Hawaiians. Lots of bad-ass characters from Nanakuli, a real tough neighborhood. Nobody messed with Nanakuli guys. They gave me a really tough time. When I first started school there, guys would spit on the ground in front of me, wherever I walked.

I finally made friends with Bongo Alapai, a giant, three-hundred-pound Hawaiian. We had wood shop together. That was one class I excelled in, but Bongo wasn't worth shit at wood. He couldn't make a thing. So I built him a doorstop to turn in for his project. He got an A, and from that time on I was his haole boy. Nobody could mess with me after that.

Little by little, I made friends with other Hawaiians and got along really well. Since then my heart has always belonged with the Hawaiians. To this day, when I go to the Islands, to the home of my good friend Henry Preece or Buffalo Keaulana, they introduce me to their friends as "Dis my good friend Greg Noll. He went Waipahu High." It gives me instant local credibility.

I had real bad sores, or kakios, on my feet from stepping on coral. The coral sand gets in your sores and gets infected. I still have the scars. At school, you had to have a permit from the nurse to wear go-aheads, or thongs, or else you had to wear shoes. Well, the nurse was an old haole gal and she liked me. I told her I just couldn't wear shoes, I've got these awful sores . . . She gave me a permanent pass to wear thongs.

In every class the teacher would ask me for a pass. If I didn't have it on me I'd go to the nurse and get another one. Pretty soon the teachers stopped asking me. As it turned out, I was the only guy who never wore shoes to school. That was my claim to fame at Waipahu High.

No Hawaiian I know likes to wear shoes, so this really pissed them off. Guys from Waipahu High still remember. Years later, whenever they see me they say, "You fockin' haole, how come I hadda wear shoes an' I never see you wear 'em even one time?"

In our quonset hut, each guy had his own shelf in the refrigerator. There were always hassles going on over who stole food from the other guy. Some peanut butter was missing from one guy's stash. Two pieces of bread from another guy's. Jelly from another.

I finally caught one guy in the act. His name was Pat McGraw, and he had just moved in with us. He didn't know I was outside, watching him through the window. He goes into the kitchen, opens up the refrigerator, takes a slice of bread from one shelf, takes some other stuff from another guy's shelf, makes himself a giant sandwich from everyone else's food. I busted him. He had us going at each other's throats all this time.

Like most teenage guys, we were a horny bunch. One time a big Samoan girl entertained seven of us. We finally had to pull Billy Ming off of her by the ankles. He was hopelessly in love. We took her underwear and I went to school the next day flying it on the antenna of my truck. The next thing we know, her big Samoan husband comes storming through our quonset hut and sends us big-shot haoles running for the hills. We all had to lie low for a couple weeks after that.

Other Recollections

MIKE STANGE

Greg and I really got to know each other in the fall of '54 when we were in the Islands for the first time. Billy Ming and I and a few other guys had spent the summer there. Greg came over around the end of August. About six of us went in together and rented an old army quonset hut out near the point at Makaha.

1954 was the beginning of a lifetime of experience for me. I'd spent my last couple years in high school dreaming about Makaha and its big waves. The North Shore was like the back side of the moon in those days. Full of mysterious and frightening tales. Makaha was the place of ridable big waves. Bobby Grubb, another of my high school buddies who was a Manhattan Beach Pier surfer, and I had stoked ourselves to a high pitch that last year of high school. Too high for me, to the detriment of schoolwork and all else. I went down the tubes in more ways than on waves, with dropped classes, failing grades and finally, expulsion from school several months before graduation.

My poor parents didn't understand what was happening to me. My older brother, who had gone through El Segundo High before me, was a great athlete and student who went on to U.C.L.A., played on several championship water polo teams and competed in the 1954 Olympics in Helsinki. And here I was, a dropout.

But Makaha did come up to twenty feet that year, so I finally got my wish. In fact, in '56, Makaha again broke at twenty feet and again I got my wish. Greg was in Australia with the lifeguard paddling team when it happened.

I met Billy Ming through Bobby Grubb while we were in high school. Bill would show up in his canary-yellow Model T pickup outside school on Thursday and we'd all head to Rincon for four or five days. These trips to Rincon developed in us a love for the place that would bring me, Ming and Greg all together again in 1955 to live near there for a time.

Billy Ming was from San Pedro. He was like a character right out of a John Steinbeck novel, real slow and easygoing, talked like a down-home boy. Bill was a good influence on us younger guys. He loved people and people loved him. He was a basic, honest guy who loved to have a good time. In the fifties, surfing was a far-out, good-time-on-the-fringes sport. People who lived ten miles inland didn't know what a surfboard was. I don't think most people today realize how fast surfing developed between 1950 and 1960.

Every summer, we'd all work as lifeguards on the Mainland to earn money to go back to Hawaii for the winter surf. In '54, I lived in the

Islands for six months on six hundred dollars I had saved during the summer. We ate a lot of oatmeal. Greg and I were actually a lot better off than a lot of the guys who went over there. Some of them didn't have any money.

Those early years at Makaha are among the highlights of my life. Our quonset hut looked right out at the point. Our daily routine revolved around surfing, diving and fishing. If the surf was flat, we'd fish or dive. If there were waves, we'd surf. School came second . . . or third. I probably averaged a few days a week, just enough to get by.

During the week, there were only a handful of guys who surfed Makaha, mostly those of us who lived there in quonset huts. George Downing would come out on weekends. Georgie grew up in the Islands. He's an all-around great waterman—paddler, swimmer and surfer. He used to come over to the Mainland to compete in paddleboard races. He was one of those surfers who was out there because he genuinely loved surfing.

To me, George Downing is an incredible individual who has made an enormous contribution to the sport. He's still out there. His kids are out there. His son, Keone, is a big-wave rider and champion surf canoe paddler in his own right. George and his family run a surf shop, and George organizes surf contests. He promotes surfing as a way of life. When I was growing up, George Downing was my idol.

Georgie was known as the Teacher. He loved seeing others get involved in surfing and was always willing to help you out, give you tips to improve your performance. He was also very competitive. But it was a healthy competition that you saw among a lot of the early big-wave surfers. Georgie's now getting the recognition he deserves.

Wally Froiseth was another great old surfer who started back in the redwood-board era. Georgie learned a lot from him. Wally was sort of Georgie's mentor when Georgie became among the first of the new breed of surfers to use lightweight boards. Georgie took advantage of the balsa-wood board and was the first to really conquer Makaha. In my opinion, George Downing was the first of the modern big-wave riders.

When Buffalo Keaulana was just a kid, he would come down from Nanakuli and stay at Makaha with different aunties and uncles. And the Kaeo brothers came to Makaha to ride their hot curl boards.

Hot curl boards are solid redwood planks with no fins. The tail comes down in a V shape, the bottom is rounded and there is no scoop in them at all. If God had granted me the foresight, I would have taken all kinds of pictures of the Kaeo brothers surfing on those hot curl boards. They are the hardest boards to ride, but they developed and forced a style on surfers that is one of the most beautiful things in the world to watch.

Gigi Kaeo and his three brothers rode their hot curl boards in a beautiful, side-slipping, superloose way. These boards went sideways as much as they went forward. You rode with one foot right behind the other. Put your weight on the back to sink that V tail, and the board would go forward. Move your weight forward a little to bring the board up, and you'd side-slip on the wave. So rather than carving turns, they would keep the board going straight, and when they wanted to slow down, they would just drop the board sideways down the face of the wave, then put their weight on the back of the board and the inside edge to go forward again. The style was very fluid, a thing of beauty to watch. It's become a lost art.

In addition to Buffalo and the Kaeo brothers, there was an old Hawaiian guy who would come out from town to bodysurf. He was about sixty, but he had the body of a thirty-year-old. We called him the Old Man. You'd be on a wave, trying to get through a tight spot, then look back at your tailblock and there was the Old Man, locked right in behind you. He was considered the best bodysurfer in the Islands. Buff was right behind him. When he was a kid, Buff couldn't afford a surfboard, so he bodysurfed. He was incredible. Buff was the first guy to ever do a bodyroll while bodysurfing.

That was our routine during the week. On weekends another eight or ten guys would show up. Mostly Hawaiians. That was when we started going to the North Shore. When we started getting a crowd of twelve or fifteen guys in the water at Makaha, we thought it was really plugged.

At that time almost the entire North Shore was taboo. Occasionally a couple guys surfed Sunset Beach, which then was called Pau Malu. There's a story that's been handed down about Woody Brown, Dickie

Cross and Wally Froiseth surfing at Sunset a few years before I first went to Hawaii. Sunset blew up on them. Absolutely closed out before they could even think to paddle in. Of course there were no helicopters in those days and they'd have been risking their lives to try to paddle in, so one of them said, "Let's try Waimea Bay." Understand, everyone was unfamiliar with the North Shore, so they would have had no idea that the Bay was not a safe harbor.

They paddled outside the few miles to Waimea and were horrified to find out that it was closed out too. But it was getting dark and they knew they had to go for it. Brown and Froiseth made it to shore—they washed up on the beach—but Cross was killed coming in. This just heightened the taboo. It wasn't until 1957 that we broke the spell and became the first to surf Waimea.

One time the surf had been flat for about two weeks at Makaha and everybody was going nuts with nothing to do—except me. I could go to school. Mike and Ming got this bright idea to walk around the island of Oahu.

They made themselves little knapsacks to carry over their shoulders, like hobos. When they got ready to leave on their trek, they were fresh-shaven, their hair was combed, they looked real neat. Mike couldn't wear shoes because his feet were full of kakios. So his feet were wrapped in gauze.

They headed out towards Kaena Point with smiles on their faces and knapsacks on their shoulders. Two days later, I was just getting home from school when I saw two bums coming my way, dragging knapsacks. I finally recognized my buddies, Mike and Ming. The gauze from Mike's feet had unraveled and was trailing behind him in the dirt. And there was something odd about their faces. As they got closer, I realized that they were red and swollen from hundreds of mosquito bites. Those buggers had cut Mike's and Ming's hike short.

I used to drive an old hearse in the Islands. When we went to the North Shore to surf, we'd sleep in it. You'd have to roll up all the windows and plug up every hole to keep out the mosquitoes. We'd get cotton balls and try to plug up every potential entryway we could find before we'd even dare try to sleep. But the little buggers would find a way—they'd get under the hood and belly-crawl up the accelerator pedal and get us every time.

45

MIKE STANGE

It was terrible. The mosquitoes drove us right into the water. They wouldn't leave us alone.

We got as far as Waialua. We had walked clear around Kaena Point with the bugs eating us and couldn't find any place to bed down. Finally this local guy took pity on us and took us to a good beach where he said we could sleep for the night.

As it turns out, there was a giant barrier of kiawe bushes on the beach, making a perfect windbreak. It was dark out there and we didn't have a flashlight. We rolled up in our blankets and before we knew it, sand crabs started crawling up our legs.

We'd jerk awake and roll around, trying to swat these crabs off our legs, then roll into the kiawe branches, right into the thorns. Then the mosquitoes started working on us again. Ming is a pretty even-tempered guy, but by the middle of the night he'd had enough. He was cursing, dancing around, trying to slap mosquitoes, swat crabs and sidestep thorns. "Let's get the hell out of here!" he said. "I can't take it anymore."

Nothing ever upset Ming, so I got alarmed when he freaked out over the mosquitoes. I knew we had to get back to Makaha before he cracked.

I guess you could say that we lived a much different lifestyle and experienced a side of Hawaii that most tourists never see.

Airfare to Hawaii was always the biggest outlay for surfers. Once you got there, there was usually someone you knew to stay with, or several guys would rent a place together.

For a few years, surfers used an airline called U.S.O.A. It was founded by an old lobster fisherman, Frank Donohue. The airfare was cheap, something like $75 one way, and the flight was horrifying. Those old DC-6s looked and sounded like they had been glued together with flour paste. It took forever to get to Hawaii. Guys would be crapped out in the aisles. You'd spend a week recovering from one of those flights.

I was publishing a surfing annual at the time. I gave Donohue an ad and he gave me a free ticket. I'm not sure now if that was a fair trade. I had to wait two days in the airport for the flight to take off. It wasn't so much that the flights were unscheduled—Donohue just wouldn't take off until there were enough passengers to make it worth it.

I heard a story about one of the regular U.S.O.A. pilots who got drunk and couldn't fly. Donohue knew how to fly, but he didn't have the credentials to fly a commercial airliner. Since he couldn't afford to give back everybody's money, Donohue climbed into the pilot's seat and took off for Hawaii. I guess the regulations were pretty thin in those days. These were such rubberband flights.

In the winter of '56, several of us decided to take a cruise ship home from Hawaii. The cruise lines were offering ridiculously low fares to compete with the increasing number of airline companies that had begun to fly to the Islands. Mickey Muñoz, Bruce Brown, Bob Sheppard, Jack Haley and I traveled on the *S.S. Leilani*. The dinner menu offered five courses, all you could eat. We wiped them out every night.

The first night, when the waiters came to our table, they asked each one of us, "And what will you have tonight, sir?" Each of us said, in turn, "Everything you've got on the menu." They brought us food by the tray- and cartload until we finished it all off.

During the day, we did calisthenics on the deck. It was a seven-day trip and there was nothing else to do. We did calisthenics for hours, working up appetites for dinner. Then we'd eat every entrée—mahimahi, steak, chicken, lobster—all the side dishes, then dessert. Towards the end of the trip, the waiter would come to the table and politely say, "I suppose you all want everything on the menu . . . again."

THE NORTH SHORE, FIRST TIME

Other Recollections

MIKE STANGE

I've never forgotten the day we drove from Makaha over to ride the North Shore for the first time. As we came up out of Wahiawa, we could see nothing but pineapple fields all the way down to Wailua and Haleiwa. The surf was rolling in from way out on the horizon. I can still remember the kind of strange and lonely feeling that came over me, knowing that something awesome was happening out there and that I was going to be a part of it, if my courage held up. If I hadn't been with Greg, I would never have gone out at Sunset or at Waimea. It was just too scary.

I have a photo of Greg at Waimea taken several years after we were the first to surf there. In the photo, he's riding the biggest wave I've ever seen anyone ride. I didn't see him ride Makaha in '69, and I'm glad I wasn't there—he probably would have talked me into going out there with him, like he did at so many other places. But I remember that set at Waimea. It was in December of '64. I had lost my board in the previous set and had to swim in, climb over the rocks to get my board. I stood up just in time to see another set come through. I couldn't believe it. It was monstrous, preternatural. And there was Greg, taking off on the biggest wave of the set and streaking across with the channel starting to break in the middle. It took my breath away. That wave looked so unbelievably big and Greg looked so unbelievably small.

At the time, I never thought about the consequences of what we were doing. My deal was "If it feels good, do it."

In life, you only get one shot at a friend like Mike Stange. He's become my closest friend, my brother. He pisses me off with his self-criticism, but I love him. Mike always has been a deep thinker and a challenging friend. He loves to argue. He reads a lot of books, listens to classical music, and, although he dropped out of school early, he's continued his education on his own. Mike had, and still has, the heart of a lion and the courage to match.

During the years that Mike was surfing with me, he was a tremendous companion. When you're headed out to an unknown place, it's a lot more fun to have someone you trust and care for beside you. During the days we surfed together, Mike often was viewed by others as my sidekick, and he likes to tell how he let me figure the lineups. Well, this may be so, but Mike was my reassurance. I benefited equally from the friendship. We became a team during those early days. There wasn't much we didn't do together. Our friendship has carried into the present, and continues to enrich my life.

One day, Mike and I just jumped in the truck and headed to the North Shore. That day is still as clear in my mind as it was then. Steve Voorhees and Jim Fisher were with us. We drove through the pineapple fields to the big taboo land. It was a beautiful day. We drove across the Haleiwa Bridge, looking for Sunset Beach. We didn't know exactly where it was; we just hoped to run into it. The surf looked good, about six or eight feet. A very small day for the North Shore, as we now realize.

We drove by all the big places that were not yet named or even known. That seven-mile stretch along the North Shore has become God's gift to surfers. I remember driving past so many beautiful breaks. Every so often, one of us would yell, "Look at that!" We had our pick of wherever we wanted to go out.

There was one place I wanted to stop and try out. It was in front of Jock Sutherland's mom's house, just the other side of Laniakea. Jock was just a toddler then, but he would grow up to be a well-known surfer. That day, everybody got pissed off because they wanted to find Sunset and I wanted to try this spot. It was my truck we were driving, but I grudgingly went on.

49

We finally agreed to stop at one place where the surf looked good. A really pretty spot. Nobody told us it was Sunset Beach. A sign nearby said PAU MALU. The name Sunset Beach came later, from a little market down the street called Sunset Market.

We went out and had a good time, got stomped on a bit. We were not at all experienced in big waves. Even six- and eight-footers were a challenge. We finally got back in the truck and headed to that spot I had originally wanted to try, by Sutherland's house. The other guys thought it looked shitty. They wanted to head back to Makaha. I went out anyway and caught three or four waves before the other guys finally came out. It was a lot better once you got out there and started surfing. In fact, that day, the waves were better than the ones we had ridden at Sunset. For about five years after that, the guys called this place Noll's Reef.

We became good friends with Mrs. Sutherland. She would invite us in for lunch now and then. This was more than a bunch of teenagers on their own from the Mainland could ask for.

MIKE STANGE

During that first trip to the North Shore, the same thing nearly happened to us that happened to Woody Brown, Dickie Cross and Wally Froiseth. The surf came up. From nice six-to-eight-foot waves, it just got bigger and bigger and bigger. We were out at the place near Sutherland's house that we called Noll's Reef and Greg saw this mountain moving across the point and said, "We gotta get back to Sunset."

Greg and Fisher and I actually went back to Sunset Beach. Here we were, just kids, and we paddled out at Sunset as it was coming up. Fisher was ahead of us and caught a wave first. Greg and I were together. We pulled off the rip and a wave came up that was the biggest thing I had ever seen. I saw Greg rise to the top of the wave—he looked like a tiny doll—just before it broke on us. I pushed my board toward the rip and dove under.

We finally struggled in to shore. The waves were still coming up and my board was still caught in the rip. Greg talked me into borrowing Fisher's board and paddling out in the rip. We started feeling scared, remembering the story about Dickie Cross. George Downing and some of the other guys had warned us to be careful on the North Shore. Now, here we were, in the thick of it.

Even the channel looked like it was going to break on us. The waves seemed to be leaping up in size. Greg suddenly says, "Let's catch some of these bigger sets that are breaking straight across! Go!"

So he catches one of those waves and I'm suddenly left out there alone. I was scared to death. I finally caught some inside shorebreaker—even it was about ten feet high—just to get in.

Afterwards, we stood on top of the truck, watching the waves break on the horizon. When we had left Makaha that morning, the waves were just lapping on shore. Now, that afternoon, we were getting our first look at close-out sets on the North Shore. The sun was going down, the spray from the waves hung like clouds on the horizon. The next morning, the entire North Shore was closed out. We went back to Makaha and it was big there, too.

My first exposure to big waves left an everlasting impression. As the waves grew in size and started breaking farther out, the ocean looked like it was tipping up on the horizon. I'll never forget it. I probably wouldn't have gone out if it hadn't been for Greg. He always encouraged me to go beyond what I thought were my capabilities.

My first season in the Islands was a real learning experience. I still had a lot of surfing to do to get to the point where I felt comfortable in big waves. I think any Mainland surfer's first exposure to the North Shore produces some ominous feelings. Surfing big waves is not something you tackle easily.

After that first time, we made four or five trips over to the North Shore that year. Hardly anyone lived there—for sure, no one we knew. In those days, when surfers went to the Islands, they stayed at Makaha. The North Shore was a remote outpost.

It's hard for surfers today to imagine what it was like, back in the fifties. When we drove to the North Shore, usually the only other surfers we'd see were the ones we took with us in the truck. In recent visits to Oahu, when I first come over the hill from Wahiawa, what I see in my mind is the isolation of the place as we knew it. Not a place crawling with people, like it is today. Today, you drive down that seven-mile stretch and see cars bumper-to-bumper at every one of those surf spots—Haleiwa, Waimea, Pupukea, Pipeline, Sunset.

The second winter we were in the Islands, we went to Sunset more often. That was also the year we discovered Haleiwa, and I met Hanalei—Henry Preece—who was to become my lifelong friend.

We had no idea during those first few winters that the North Shore would become the surf center of the planet Earth. We were just kids, blundering along. I was learning about surfing big waves and getting hooked on them. All this time, Waimea was waiting for me.

HALEIWA, HENRY AND BUFF

Those first couple of winters, we didn't even know that Haleiwa existed as a surf spot. We had been going to Sunset and Noll's Reef a lot that second winter. On the way back to Makaha, we always drove through Haleiwa.

One afternoon, we were driving across the bridge at Haleiwa and I happened to notice that there was someone out in the water. I could see that he was Hawaiian and he was taking off on a neat little wave. We had never noticed any surf at Haleiwa, so we decided to try to find a way out there, to solve the mystery. We turned right at the Seaview Inn, on the road that heads out towards Kaena Point. We had never gone this way before.

Today, there's a beach park at the site, but at that time, there were solid kiawe bushes between the road and the beach. No road leading in. The water was hardly visible except for that one spot off the bridge. We parked on the side of the road and cautiously made our way through the thorny kiawe, trying to find a path to the beach. A couple of farmers had their cows grazing there and we discovered one little cowpath that led to the beach. We stepped out of the bushes and felt like we had emerged into Shangri-La.

Here was a beautiful new surf spot and one lone Hawaiian, sitting out in the water on his surfboard, waving to us to come join him, glad to have some company. Any surfer today who found a spot like this would never tell anybody about it.

Up until then, I had never met Henry Preece. I had seen him once before at Makaha, but I had never talked to him. Both Henry and Buffalo Keaulana grew up in the Nanakuli area. Buffalo stayed, but Henry

53

supposedly had been run out after giving one of the Nanakuli girls a big opou. While the girl's mother was beating the bushes in Nanakuli, looking for Henry, he took off to Haleiwa to conquer new ground.

We paddled out to join him. It was about two in the afternoon, and we had an absolutely memorable time. The surf was perfect. The three of us surfed our guts out. Until our arms wouldn't work anymore.

Henry invited us to his house afterwards. He lived in a little eight-by-ten shack on the beach at Haleiwa that he had made out of scrap wood with tin for the roof and empty Kotex boxes for siding. It was a shack, but it was immaculate. Henry is an immaculate guy, and everything was, in its own primitive way, absolute perfection.

He cranked up his Coleman lantern, filled a pot with seawater and made rice in it. Made some stuff he called moi, out of canned sardines, onions, different seasonings and God knows what else. Of course, after surfing so hard, the food tasted better than anything in the world. We spent the night right there in Henry's shack. The next morning, we surfed Haleiwa with him again.

Since then, Hanalei—that's Hawaiian for Henry—has become like a brother to me. When I go back to the Islands, I charge straight to Henry's house for a beer. My family and I always stay there. I've made more than forty trips to the Islands and have sometimes stayed at Henry's house for three months at a crack.

On one particular evening, Hanalei and I were raising hell together. We had recently watched an old movie where a cowboy and an Indian had cut their wrists and become blood brothers. Hanalei grabbed a pointed beer can opener and we ended up becoming haole and Hawaiian blood brothers. Twenty years later, we both still have the scars to prove it.

There are old surf movies that show Henry Preece riding Haleiwa. He seemed to have a special rapport with that spot. As he grew older, Henry stopped surfing regularly for many years. He took up golf and plays very well. Now some of his grandchildren have begun surfing, so he has started going out with them. At Haleiwa.

We call Henry the Mayor of Haleiwa. All the locals know him, know where he lives. He and his buddies formed a little group and play Hawaiian music at weddings and parties. They call themselves the Nobodies. Henry worked for years for the county. He may not be as widely known as Buffalo Keaulana is for his surfing and paddling accomplishments, but to me Hanalei is a living example of the Aloha Spirit. A warm and friendly person and one of my closest amigos.

If Hanalei is the Mayor of Haleiwa, then Buff is certainly the Mayor of Makaha. I don't think I'm stretching the truth when I say that Buff is considered by many people in Hawaii to be the one Hawaiian most likely to take Duke Kahanamoku's place. The guy is a classic. If he'd been born two hundred years ago, he'd have been a Hawaiian king. They just broke the mold with Buff.

His name is Richard Keaulana, but he's called Buffalo because of his shaggy, reddish-brown hair. I'm sure some of his Hawaiian ancestors could be traced back to the time of Captain Cook.

Buffalo looks like he belongs to the ocean. I remember one time we were drinking and messing around down at Yokohama Bay, just above Makaha. It was a hot day and Buff got up and walked down to the water to cool off and do some bodysurfing. At one time, Buff was considered to be the best bodysurfer in Hawaii. That day, there was about a six-foot shorebreak and he was there, silhouetted in the sun against those waves. Just streaking across them, like a seal. He looked so natural, like he should have turned and swam out to sea when he was done.

Buff was the first lifeguard at Makaha. For years, they had no such thing. When the state made Makaha into a beach park, Buff was so well known at Makaha there was no question about who would be suitable as lifeguard. Besides, if a fight broke out, he was the only one respected enough to be able to stop it. He spent nineteen years as lifeguard there. Since then, he's been parkkeeper. His kids surf. His sons, Brian and Rusty, are rated among the top pro surfers and paddlers. Brian is probably the top big-wave rider at Makaha today.

To Buff's kids, I'm Uncle, just as Buff and Henry are Uncle to my kids. Brian and Rusty love to remind me of the time when I had slept overnight on the lower bunk of their bed. They were just little farts then and they woke me up in the morning, pissing on me from the top bunk.

Like all well-known people, Buff is somewhat aware of the aura that he projects. Very natural, very native. People are naturally attracted to him. Many years ago I was at his house when this guy arrived for a visit. Later I find out that this "guy" was the commander of the entire naval fleet in Pearl Harbor. He lived out near Makaha and had gotten to know Buff. While Buff is introducing me as one of his other haole friends, the phone rings. It's for the commander. The navy was calling to get clearance from him to take out an aircraft carrier.

One of Buff's kids started squealing, and Buff says to the commander, "Here, hold Baby." Just plops the kid in the commander's lap. At first I was blown away. Here's this guy who causes men to snap their heels together and salute, holding a crying baby with messy diapers while Buff goes out to the kitchen to get some old piece of fish from the refrigerator. But the commander is drinking beer and eating fish and holding Baby and loving every minute of it. At Buff's, you get treated the same as everyone else, no matter who you are. I guess this is why the commander liked to visit.

Henry and Buff rarely leave the Islands. Henry was supposed to come visit me a couple years ago. He had gone with a golf team from the Islands to Las Vegas for a tournament and was supposed to swing by my place on his way back. He called me and said, "Brudda, no can come. Gotta go home." Hawaiians are good for about three days on the Mainland before they cave in with homesickness. They're very family-oriented.

Buff is a little better about travel since he's had more exposure as a celebrity. One year I took Buff and the Hawaiian surf team to the old Long Beach Pike amusement park after they came back from competing in the world championships in Peru. We rode on the bumper cars, the ferris wheel and the rollercoaster. They had never done anything like this and they loved it. Buff and Chubby Mitchell were in the front and Freddie Hemmings and I were behind them. As the cars are being pulled up the first long hill, Buff and Chubby are giggling and saying, "Hey, dis not so bad!" When the track fell away and the car plunged straight down, their giggles turned to screams. We accused Chubby of bending the steel bar, he held on so tight.

To top off the day, I took them to a topless bar. I thought Buff would lose it then and there. He couldn't get his eyes off the gals' tits long enough to order a beer.

Other Recollections

HENRY PREECE

One day, Buff and Greg tell me, "We make cake for you." I think, "Nice!" I eat it, pass out. Woke up, had no clothes on. Find out later it was pakalolo [marijuana] cake.

Another time, we all meet at bar, get ripped. Greg pass me plate of puu puus. I pick up one, about silver-dollar size. I start rolling it around in my mouth. "What dis?" I ask Greg. "Aku eye," he say. Nice guy.

I eat almost anything, so Greg always bringing me food. I was on chili pepper kick for a while, so Greg bring me some peppers from Mexico. So hot, make me dance around for half an hour! Then I try to catch Greg, but he too fast. I got serious mad. Not talk to Greg for three days.

I love dis guy, but I like choke his neck once in a while. After thirty years plus, what else can I do? I run out of stories, I get sick of lookin' at him, but I miss dis guy a lot when he not here.

Over the years, Henry and Buff and I have become like brothers. You don't see many relationships like ours today in Hawaii. Haoles go over there and live in haole areas, like out around Pipeline, where most of the real estate has been bought by haoles. The haoles stick together; the Hawaiians stick together. There isn't much cross-association.

In my time, surfing was the common denominator that brought us all together. When you're young, the people you share growing experiences with are the one who make the biggest impact on your life. You carry those experiences, those relationships, with you throughout your life. I met Henry and Buff during a period in my life when I was young, breaking away and stumbling along, trying to figure out, "Who is Greg Noll?"

Because I share such deep, strong ties with Henry and Buff, I feel a lot of empathy for most Hawaiians. I don't like to see them get stepped on and I don't like to see the bad press they sometimes get from trying to protect what is theirs. On several occasions I've been caught right in the middle of that crossfire and gotten my ass kicked by Hawaiians. I didn't like it, but I understood it. I'd get up the next day, lick my wounds and go right back out and have a drink with them.

I met Buffalo the first year I went to Hawaii. He was nineteen, a couple years older than the rest of us. You couldn't get two words out of him. He was the quietest person I had ever met, which is very unlike his personality now.

He would just grunt when we spoke to him, or he'd talk in two-word sentences. We just didn't know what to make of the guy. We could see that he was a great waterman. You could already see it coming out of him. We just naturally gravitated towards him.

Buff didn't own a surfboard. He would borrow one of ours. We sometimes wondered if that was the only reason he hung around us. I really started to get to know him better after a paddle race that all of us entered.

Paddling contests were part of an event called Aloha Days in Waikiki. Mike Bright—Bones—had joined us in Makaha to compete in the Diamond Head race. He and I had done a lot of paddling on the Mainland, so we decided to enter some of the Aloha Days events. We asked Buffalo to go, too. He said, "I no like go."

Come to find out, Buff had never been to Waikiki in his whole young life. In fact, he had never even been beyond Barber's Point. Bones and I finally talked Buff into going and we all piled in my old car with our boards and went to town. Buff felt so uncomfortable in Waikiki. He was so shy, he wouldn't talk to anybody. I had to fill out his entry form, register him for the event.

We all won something that day. I can't remember what, exactly, because the biggest prize turned out to be Buff's friendship. On the drive back to Makaha, we stopped to get some food. I bought Buff a hamburger. He grunted. We get to Nanakuli, Buff says, "My auntie live ova dere," so I drove up into the hills and dropped him off at his auntie's house. He gets out of the car. Never even looks over his shoulder, never says anything, just walks into the house and closes the door. Bones and I look at each other: "Jeez, you ever seen a guy like that before?"

Four or five days later, a couple carloads of Hawaiians roll up in front of our quonset hut. Out steps Buff, leading a procession of his friends with two cases of beer and all kinds of food. It meant a lot to him to win a contest and this was his way of showing us his appreciation. That year, before I went home, I gave Buff my board. His first board. From that point on, Buff and I were close friends.

Buff soon came into his own as a surfer. A few years after that, he got drafted and stationed in Haleiwa. By then, I was concentrating on the North Shore and living over there instead of staying in Makaha. So now the three of us were together. I was at Henry's house and Buff was only a few blocks away at the Haleiwa Army Beach. He was the lifeguard and in charge of the grounds. What else could the Army do with Buff? He wouldn't be worth a damn anywhere else but in the Islands.

Buff became very friendly with all the officers. When there were parties at the Officers' Club, Buff would hold back some food and drink, then slip us in after the party. Sometimes, late at night, we'd go out on the base grounds in our old car and try to pop toads. Buff hung off one fender and Henry hung off the other, spotting toads, while I drove back and forth trying to hit the damn things. They make a really neat popping sound when you hit one. The following morning, the high muckamucks would come on base and see these flat toads all over the place. I don't know if they ever figured out who squashed them.

Other Recollections

BUFFALO KEAULANA

One day, I go scuba diving with Greg and my Chinese friend Norman Mau. On the way out, we're talkin' up some shark stories. We come by Yokohama Bay and anchor about half a mile out in about seventy to eighty feet of water. We there to pick up lobsters.

We gear up, with Greg on port side and me on starboard. At count of three, both of us supposed to let go of the boat and jump in the water. We reach the count of three, Greg let go of the boat. But I stay there, still checkin' everything.

Greg go down about two feet, then he go under the boat to see if I also underwater. He come up on the boat railing and see me. I look him straight in the eye and say, "Anybody stay home?" meaning, "Any sharks?"

From then on, Greg never go in water diving unless I go first. Now we both look at each other, say, "Anyboooody?" One who goes in first has to find out if anybody stay home.

Henry sent his daughter, Pumohala, to live with me and my family when she was in high school. She is a beautiful Hawaiian girl with hair so black it looks purple in the sunlight. She also was a typical, shy Hawaiian

59

country girl. The word *shy* means nothing until you've met a shy Hawaiian country girl. She didn't talk for three days. At the time, Beverly and I lived near Hermosa Beach. Pumo spent a semester with us, and, as a result, she really matured and gained some self-confidence. After she went home, she joined a Tahitian dance group that later toured Japan and the South Pacific. To this day, I consider her my second daughter.

Buff and his wife, Momie, have five children of their own. But Buff's family is very extended. Buff is always surrounded by an entourage of guys who surf Makaha. He's always taking in several kids at a time. They sleep and eat there, then drift off after a while.

Nowadays you don't go surfing at Makaha unless you know someone local and they're with you. One time, I had my two older sons with me in the Islands, and they told me that they wanted to surf Makaha. Their Uncle Buff said to his son Brian, "Take da boys." As they were waxing up their boards on the beach, three or four local guys started to give the boys the frog-eye. Then they saw Brian, who said, "Hey, these my haoles." The locals left them alone.

A couple of years ago, my daughter, Ashlyne, went tandem surfing at Makaha with Brian. He's one of the best tandem riders in the Islands. Brian's regular partner was out of commission, so he was trying out new girls. To be chosen as Brian's tandem partner is a real honor for local girls, so Ashlyne was really proud to get the opportunity.

Buff's and Henry's generation is really the last of the true Hawaiians. In the process of modernizing, each generation gains a little distance from its cultural heritage. The best way I can describe it is that when I'm in the Islands and we go someplace with Hawaiian kids, they tune the radio to rock 'n' roll. When Buff and I drive someplace, he tunes to Hawaiian music.

Wherever Buff goes, he ends up with a captivated audience listening to him "talk stories." Buff was part of the team that sailed four thousand miles from Hawaii to Tahiti in the outrigger *Hokule'a,* navigating only by stars. He's been to Japan, Peru and other places in the world to promote surfing or paddling. He's been elevated to celebrity status, but get a few beers in him and he's still the same kid that went to Waikiki with us for the first time, so many years ago.

Although Mike Stange and I spent a lot of time together in the Islands, living with different guys who had also come over from the Mainland to surf, a lot of my spare time was spent with the local

Hawaiians. As a result of my friendship with Henry and Buff, several other local Hawaiians became interested in surfing and asked me to make boards for them.

All the guys chipped in for materials. I bought enough balsa wood from McGwain's Marine Store in Waikiki to make about ten boards. We set up the wood on sawhorses outside of Henry's shack at Haleiwa. I used a hand planer and a drawknife. Balsa shavings were blowing in the wind all the way down to the Haleiwa Bridge. At any given time, there must have been about thirty Hawaiians there, watching and helping. We even glassed the boards inside the shack. It turned into sort of a community project.

I had no idea what the far-reaching results of this goodwill gesture would be. The Hawaiians were, and are, very appreciative of things like this. A few of the guys still have their boards and never miss a chance to let people know: "I have one of the original Greg Noll boards that were shaped at Haleiwa." It was a big deal and it gave the Hawaiians a few surfboards that they could really surf on, rather than using some of those old junk redwoods they had been riding.

This all happened thirty years ago, when Haleiwa Beach Park was just a mess of kiawe bushes and cow trails. Today, whenever I take my kids there, they see a long, sandy beach. I see it as I did when I was trying to hack my way through the growth to get to the water where I had seen that lone Hawaiian, Hanalei, on a wave and backlit in the afternoon sun.

One of my proudest accomplishments in making surfboards was making signature boards for Duke Kahanamoku. The board was called the Duke Kahanamoku Nollrider and commemorated the Duke Kahanamoku Invitational Surfing Championships, which were started in 1965. The Duke was an Olympic swimming champion, an all-around great waterman and the absolute embodiment of Hawaiian charm and spirit. In 1967, after I had finished an order of these boards, one of his friends asked me if there was anything I wanted from the Duke. I told him that I'd love to have something I could keep, something inscribed. A couple of months later, I made a trip to the Islands and was given a wristwatch inscribed "TO GREG, FROM DUKE, 1967." This was just before the Duke died.

OF PADDLERS AND LIFEGUARDS

A lot of early surfers like myself started out lifeguarding and paddle-board racing. I entered my first paddling race when I was thirteen, along with Bing Copeland, Bev Morgan and the Meistrell brothers. We all won our class.

I was eighteen when I entered the first Catalina to Manhattan Beach Rough Water Paddleboard Race in 1955. The race started in Catalina. Each paddler was followed by a boat for the entire thirty-two-mile distance. They hand you food and drink on a pole while you're out in the water on your paddleboard, so that you don't have any contact with the boat. My boat got screwed up—the captain didn't think any of us would make it anyway—and we ended up off-course. We recalculated the distance. As it turned out, I paddled 52 miles that day. Lost nine pounds, but came in second.

Ricky Grigg beat me. His boat had a directional finder that bombed him right in.

Other Recollections

RICKY GRIGG

I was around seventeen when I won the Catalina race. They took a picture of the first six finishers with the trophies all lined up in front of us. It was George Downing, Tommy Zahn, Charlie Reimers, Bob Hogan, Noll and me, all standing there together, and there was one muscular guy

62

who was flexing. Guess who. The rest of us were so tired, we were just hanging there. Greg would just gag me. He was always hamming it up.

Greg once passed me in a race going so fast that I felt like I was going the other direction. He just streaked by me. It was ridiculous. I was ahead at that point, and the next thing I knew, he was fifty yards ahead of me. Came out of nowhere. I don't know what he was doing, but he was doing it fast.

When we started going to Hawaii for the winter surf, lifeguarding gave us the means. We'd work through the rest of the year and save as much money as we could to live on in Hawaii. As lifeguards we were dedicated to two things: making rescues and having fun. When it was time to work, rescues were taken very seriously. The rest of the time we screwed around. You can't get away with that anymore. Today you're supposed to be serious all the time.

The lifeguards I worked with had formed a club, the Wet Noodle Club. They'd give out different awards for various stupid things. My initiation into the club happened at a time when I was working for a head lifeguard by the name of John Horne, a real serious type. We were always getting on each other's nerves.

It happened one day in the fall. I had somehow managed to split my trunks. Apparently the split exposed some of my youthful exuberance, and Horne was less than amused. He called me out of the water on the P.A. system. I calmly walked over to his truck and he read me the riot act.

"We are not going to let that get started around here," he says.

"Let what get started, sir?"

"Showing an excess of pubic hairs." We also went nose to nose over how low my trunks were hanging. Hell, I was young and cocky and always wore my trunks as if they were ready to fall off.

This incident gave my lifeguard buddies the opportunity to present Horne with a Wet Noodle Award. They tabbed him as Captain Pube-Checker and gave him a plaque with various specimens of pubic hair glued to a chart that told how much could be showing, according to your age. There was also a gauge that fit in your belly button and showed how low your trunks could be worn. It was a humiliating award that got a lot of laughs. After this, Horne and I got along great.

On occasion, rescues could be nasty. One happened at Manhattan Beach. Two guys and a girl were out in the waves and got caught in a giant rip. One of the guys was swept away from the other two. I had no backup that day and had to choose which to save. I figured two lives were better than one and started swimming out towards the girl and guy. As I swam out, I kept my eye on all three of them. Just before I'd dive under a wave, I'd see two people over here, and one person over there. After a couple waves, I came up and saw two people over here and blank over there. What a hollow feeling that gives you. Where there was a person, now there was just whitewater. That day still haunts me occasionally.

Another rescue happened at Waimea Bay before they had regular lifeguards there. I happened to be there, checking out the surf. Four sailors on leave had swam out. They got caught in the rip and were being sucked out to the middle of the Bay. The surf had started coming up and they were being swept towards the rocks. They couldn't get back in through the rip and the waves because, of course, they weren't familiar with Waimea Bay. I saw from the beach that they were in trouble, so I grabbed my board and paddled out. They were pretty happy to see me. I rounded up all four of them and told them to hold onto the back of my board and one on each leg while I paddled back in. It took us a half-hour to clear the rip and reach shore.

These guys were so relieved and happy to be alive, they kept thanking me over and over again. I finally said, "That's O.K., you can buy me a beer." They laughed, and one of the guys said, "Man, if I had the money, I'd buy you a whole brewery!"

The next day, the *Honolulu Star* ran an article on the rescue and the navy declared Waimea Bay off-limits to over three thousand sailors on Oahu. Years later they made Waimea Bay a state park with lifeguards. Up until then a few people were lost there every year.

One year, Mike Stange and I were staying in the Pupukea area. We were loading up our boards and noticed that the guy next door was out pumping up a raft. The surf was coming up. Mike said, "That guy shouldn't be taking that damn raft out today." Mike went over and tried his best to discourage him, but the guy wasn't listening to any of it. We weren't at Sunset Beach forty-five minutes when we heard the sirens screaming at Pupukea. We both kicked ourselves for not trying harder to reason with him. The guy was gone.

LAURA

There was one rescue that only a few people know about. Greg was out at Makaha and noticed that a young boy, about ten, was in trouble. Greg quickly paddled over to the boy and took him to shore on his board. A few months later, a woman and her son arrived at the factory in Hermosa Beach with a package for Greg. They went into his office. The boy handed Greg the package and said, "Thanks for saving me that day. I would have drowned if you hadn't helped me."

Inside the box was a small bronze bull.

RINCON WINTER

MIKE STANGE

In 1955, after working another season on the beach but being laid off around October, Greg, Billy Ming, Jim Fisher and I decided to spend a winter in the Santa Barbara area, near Rincon. We rented a house in Carpinteria and had a great winter of surfing. Bobby Patterson and Mickey Muñoz visited frequently, and during the week, the six of us shared day after day of perfectly shaped six-to-eight-foot waves.

Those were carefree, happy times. It was like having a whole era to ourselves. Sea, air and landscape in a dreamy passing of days spent riding waves and reflecting upon the goodness of life at this stage, living with just the basics. For me the poetry of days has never equaled that time. The early years in the Islands had drama and dimension and certainly were adventurous. But 1955 was sheer poetry—halcyon days, looking at them now from a tranquil distance.

Rincon, 1955. Midnight raids on the squash fields. The house so full of produce you couldn't walk through it. Glassing a board on the antique table of an old English guy named Floyd—somebody got shit-faced and shot up the house. Fisher and his hearse with the chicken on the roof. All these images come back to me in a blur when I think about our winter in Rincon.

But Billy Ming. How could anyone forget him? Billy Ming was a good ol' San Pedro boy. Totally unflappable. He really had the gift of gab, came across like a real hayseed. He called everything "she" or "her." Everybody who ever knew him loved him. Especially the ladies. He was a real hit with the ladies.

While we were in Rincon, we'd drive around in Billy's beat-up, rusted-out old car. He'd never make a full stop at a stop sign. He didn't want to wear out the brakes, so he'd shift down to second gear, coast up to the stop sign and roll on through. And he never drove the damn thing over twenty-five.

Except for one time, and we got pulled over by a cop. The cop comes up to the window and asks for Ming's license and registration. Of course, all Ming had on him was a pair of shorts and sandals. He never carried anything else on him, not even identification.

Even though we'd rented a house together, Ming practically lived out of his car. It was full of junk, under the seat, on the floor, in the glove box. He told the cop in his country-boy accent, "I know she's in here someplace," and started rummaging around. Ming pulls a pair of pants out from under the seat and hands them to Mike. He reaches back into the back seat and comes up with a snorkel and mask and hands those to me. By this time he's edged his way out of the car so he can grub around in the junk on the floor.

Meanwhile, Mike and I could see that the cop was getting a little amused. He's standing there, patiently, while Ming keeps pulling all this crap out of the car and piling it on top of me and Mike. "I know she's here somewheres," he'd say, and rummage around some more.

He finds his army discharge papers and reads those to the cop. No go. So Ming crawls back into the car again, pulling out more piles of junk. "Gosh, she's got to be here." After several minutes of this routine, even the cop is holding a pile of Ming's stuff. The cop finally calls a halt.

"I tell you what you'd better do," he says. "You'd better get back in *her* and start *her* up and you'd better get *her* the hell out of here before I start writing *her* up. Because I won't stop writing for a week!"

He didn't have to tell us twice. We were out of there in a flash. We looked back at the cop. He had pushed his hat back on his head and was laughing as he watched us drive away.

67

Ming even had a way with the Japanese people, who were known to be just about as serious and quiet as a person can be. Hard to get a laugh out of them. In Hawaii, Ming would go into those little mamasan and papasan grocery stores, all grinning and friendly-like. "Howdy there! How're you doin' today? You got any sody-pop? Any cream cherry sody-pop?" And he'd get them going. Have them laughing and in tears in no time.

When Ming quit surfing, he moved to Santa Barbara and became a caretaker on the Hammond Estate. He was there for years. Then he started fishing out of Santa Barbara. By this time I'd become a commercial fisherman in Crescent City, and I started hearing these stories drift up about a fellow in Santa Barbara, name of Billy Ming, doing all these outrageous things.

There was a story about how they were turning part of the harbor there in Santa Barbara into plastic boat slips that they could rent for outrageous prices. The story had it that the inspectors were pissed off because the commercial boats were stinky and the skippers were always late paying their slip fees. The inspectors wanted them cleaned up or out of there so they could get their boat-slip rental money.

Well, Ming's got this little commercial fishing boat moored there and these inspectors come down, dressed up all official, and they start telling Ming that he can't do this and he can't do that and he has to start doing this . . . Ming's boat looks like his old car, just full of crap. These guys are standing there in their suits and holding their clipboards, reading Ming the riot act. So Ming decides to start up his engine. It fires up and belches black soot and crap into the air, all over these guys. Ming stands there with a sad look on his face, "Gee guys, sorry 'bout that."

I heard another story about Ming going to the doctor for skin cancer treatment. The doctor tells him to stay out of the sun, to wear protective clothing. Commercial fishing being somewhat of an outdoor occupation, the next time Ming goes out he's wearing a wide-brimmed sun hat, gloves and gobs of sun protection cream. He's pulling up these monstrous crab traps. At first the other guys couldn't believe it was Ming. They asked, "Bill, what are ya all dressed up for?" And Ming'd say, "Ah, it's just my new outfit. I got a little skin cancer is all and I gotta stay out of the sun." No big deal, to Ming.

Ming always had some sort of rotten hound dog with him. He wrote an article for some commercial fisher magazine, claiming that his dog could smell fish. Apparently, this dog would get up in the bow and when the boat was over the fishing grounds the dog would bark. A real bullshit deal. We read this and figured it was a misprint. His dog couldn't smell fish, his dog smelled *like* fish.

ADVENTURES DOWN UNDER

In 1956 I was one of the lifeguards on the American paddling team that was invited to participate in the surf paddling contests being held during the Olympics in Melbourne, Australia. For me, at age nineteen, the trip became one in a series of firsts.

After having revived the sport in Hawaii, Duke Kahanamoku had introduced surfing to Australia at Manly Beach, Sydney, in 1915, and introduced it to both coasts in the United States. Australian lifeguards picked up the sport and used the long planks for rescue craft. By 1956 they had graduated to hollow surf skis that were all but impossible to stand on.

Tommy Zahn, Mike Bright, Bobby Moore and I paid the extra freight to take our surfboards with us to Australia. By that time we had graduated from redwoods to the shorter, lighter balsa-wood boards. We had come to race paddleboards. As it turned out, our surfboards became the real attraction. When the boards were first taken off the airplane and put on a flatbed truck, a head honcho from one of the surf clubs in Australia came over to look at them.

"What are these for, mate?" he asked us. I told him that we surfed on them. He couldn't figure it out. To him, the boards were flat and funny-looking. Up to that time, the Aussies had used a surf ski type of board, and the idea was to go out and take off on some whitewater and come straight in in the soup, while all the girls on the beach squealed. That was their idea of surfing.

This guy kept looking at the boards, touching them, turning them over. He finally said, "Give ya two bob for the works, mate." His way of saying they were worthless.

We intended to take the boards with us to the paddle meets and, during our time off, try out the Australian surf. I had bought a Bell and Howell movie camera from Warren Miller. He was just getting into making ski movies then and is still grinding them out today. I thought it would be fun to show everybody back home what Australian surf looked like.

During one event, we had noticed a little point break off to the side, off a rocky point. I don't remember the name of the place. After the paddling events were over, we grabbed our boards and paddled out to the break. There had been thousands of people watching the paddling events from shore, and they had started leaving. Ampol Oil was covering all the paddling events, and decided to stay and take films of us surfing. Word got around in the parking lot as people were leaving, "The Yanks are surfing, you ought to see the Yanks."

People turned around and came back to watch. An enormous crowd formed. Ampol Oil took films. When we left Australia, we also left our boards for the Aussies. Those films were shown all over the country to different clubs. The films and our boards became the basis for the modern surfboard movement in Australia.

The idea of finding a surf spot in a remote area was not what it was all about in Australia in those days. As we traveled from one meet to another, we saw several great-looking places along the way. I remember one spot we passed. You looked down off a cliff and about a mile away there were these beautiful lines stacked up, wave after wave. We were riding in the back of a truck with our boards and I started pounding on the cab with my fist. The driver, an Aussie, stopped and asked me, "What's the matter, mate?"

I said, "Jesus Christ, look at that surf down there! Has anyone ever surfed it?" The guy thought I was crazy. He said, "Why would anyone want to go down there?" Like, there wasn't a surf club down there, so what's the point? He refused to drive us there. Today that spot is a well-known surf spot—Long's Reef, I think they call it.

For about two years after that trip I got letters every week from guys in Australia, pleading for pictures, templates, design information. It was a new frontier for them. By then I was making boards, but it was too expensive to ship them down there. I stayed in contact with one guy for a while, sent him templates. Took pictures of boards from the top, bottom, sideways, rear. Made all sorts of notes. It didn't take the Australians long to get on with the thing. The end result is that they have since produced some of the best surfers in the world.

From the movies I took, I made my own surf film. That helped get surfers up here interested in surfing down there. Before that there wasn't any traffic back and forth between Australian and American surfers.

I often wondered, as time went by, whether the Aussies would rewrite history to suit themselves or give credit to the Californians who introduced them to the modern surfboard. A couple years ago I happened to be standing behind a guy in the airport who was struggling with a bunch of bags, so I gave him a hand. He said, in a recognizable Aussie accent, "Thanks, mate."

We got to talking and, as it turns out, this guy remembers the trip the Yanks made down there in '56. He tells me that one of the original boards is still hanging in his club. We end up having a couple of beers in the bar and talking stories until we have to go our separate ways.

That wasn't the only "first" that came out of my trip to Australia. I got to know the Australians pretty well. Fell right in with them, in fact. Hell, I was young and liked to have a good time. I almost got sent home for screwing around. One night will always remain particularly memorable: no less than five different ladies decided to bestow their warm, Australian hospitality on this poor ol' Yank. To this day, I have never received such a warm welcome, not even in my own native land of California.

My Australian buddies egged me on. I was running from one camp to another and failed to notice a two-foot-high fence that was used to corral sheep. I hit the barbed wire, fell on my ass, got sheep shit in the cut and two days later I had a red line running right up to my crotch. I ended up with blood poisoning and almost lost my leg. That's what I get for being such a horny guy.

We had to go from Melbourne to Sidney for one meet. Our guys were supposed to go by train. I got separated from the team and ended up with the Australians again. We were a mess. We hit every pub along the way. The Australians were like Hawaiians when it came to drinking. They just couldn't pass up a pub. We ended up getting totally wiped out.

It was three days before I met up with my team. By then I had cut the U.S.A. patches off my clothes and traded them with the Australians. Their logo was the Gladstone Gander holding a mug of beer. I really liked the Australians and later considered moving down there.

So here I am at the railway station to meet the team. I walked up to our coach, smelling like beer, wearing three days' growth of beard and a beer mug on my arm. Coach just shook his head and turned away. "Goddammit, if I didn't need you on the team, I'd send you home on the next airplane."

The Aussies are the most competitive guys in the world. They'll compete over anything. At an award banquet they held for us, they got me off into a corner and into a beer-drinking contest. They had their best guy there, who, little did I know, had never lost one of these contests. I was in trouble. They had some deal where they'd flip three coins to see whose turn it was to drink a big pewter schooner of beer. I don't know how it works. All I know is I lost three times in a row.

By this time a crowd of guys had gathered around to watch the Yank lose. I ran out of room for beer. It came back up and out all over the floor in front of the whole gang. I fetched a mop from the corner and cleaned up the floor. Then I drank the rest of the beer from my mug. The Aussies were cheering away. They loved it, thought it was the craziest thing they'd ever seen.

I like to think that, in my own way, I did a little towards improving our relations with the Aussies.

Other Recollections

SONNY VARDEMAN

I went to Australia in 1985 with our lifeguard team. One of the Aussies gave a talk to our group about how he remembered the first U.S. team that had come down in '56 to a club on the outskirts of Melbourne called the Torquay Surf Club. He told about how the Yanks had come down there with what they called Malibu boards. He said that these guys paddled out into the surf in front of the club for what everyone thought was a casual workout. Then they started catching waves, riding them towards shore, turning, cutting back, kicking out of a wave and paddling back out for more. All the club members went out on the beach to watch. Within two hours the word had spread and the crowd eventually grew to about ten thousand spectators, spread along the shoreline, watching the Yanks ride their boards.

The lifeguard competition has since become a regular exchange every four years. Sure, Greg got into trouble. That's the Australian way, and things haven't changed a bit. But we've learned from Greg's experiences. Today, we older lifeguards chaperone the young competitors to make sure they don't go off with the Aussies.

WAIMEA BAY, FIRST TIME

There was fierce competition, on a friendly basis, of course, among the big-wave riders: Peter Cole, Pat Curren, Mike Stange, José Angel, Ricky Grigg, Buzzy Trent, George Downing and myself. This was the nucleus of guys during my time who really enjoyed riding big waves. Each guy had his own personality and his own deal.

Downing and Trent had helped establish Makaha as the No. 1 big-wave or any-size-wave spot in the Islands. Up to this time, the winter of 1957, no one had ever ridden Waimea. For three years I had driven by the place on my way to surf Sunset Beach. I would stop the car to look at Waimea Bay. If there were waves, I'd hop up and down, trying to convince the other guys, and myself, that Waimea was the thing to do. All the time, I was trying to build up my own confidence.

At that time the North Shore was largely unexplored territory. We were kids who had heard nothing but taboo-related stories about Waimea. There was a house that all the locals believed was haunted. There were sacred Hawaiian ruins up in Waimea Canyon. And of course, the mystique of Dickie Cross dying there. We'd drive by and see these big, beautiful grinders . . . but the taboos were still too strong.

The forbiddenness of the place is what made Waimea Bay so compelling. I wanted to try it but didn't have the balls to go out by myself. So I kept promoting the idea of breaking the Bay. Buzzy Trent, my main opponent, started calling me the Pied Piper of Waimea. He said, "Follow Greg Noll and he'll lead you off the edge of the world. You'll all drown like rats if you listen to the Pied Piper of Waimea Bay."

One day in November, we stopped at Waimea just to take a look. I finally jerked my board off the top of the car and did it. Mike went with me. We were the first in the water. I was the first to catch a wave. I had paddled for one outside and missed it, so I took off on a small inside wave. By then the other guys had come in too. Pat Curren and I rode the next big wave together. And that was it. It was simple. The ocean didn't swallow us up, and the world didn't stop turning. That was how Waimea got busted. By me, Mike Stange, Mickey Muñoz, Pat Curren, Bing Copeland, Del Cannon and Bob Bermell.

Within minutes, word spread into Haleiwa that Waimea Bay was being ridden. We looked across the point and saw cars and people lining up along the road watching the crazy haoles riding Waimea Bay. There must have been a hundred people—a big crowd for that time.

To this day, when I go into Haleiwa, I stop at a little gas station that sits just before the bridge. There's an old man there who sold us gas when we were kids. He laughs whenever he sees me because we used to buy his drain oil to put in the old junk cars that we drove. The engines were gone anyway. All we wanted was to get three or four months' use out of them. Now when he sees me coming he says, "Greg Noll, I remember first time when you ride Waimea, you crazy damn haole you."

The irony of it all was, it wasn't a very big day by Waimea standards. Just nice-shaped waves. I spun out on one wave and wrenched my shoulder. It's still screwed up from that first day at Waimea. We were using ridiculous equipment, boards that we had brought over from the Mainland. Definitely not made for big waves. We had a long ways to go in big-wave riding and big-wave-board design.

When we first surfed Waimea, we weren't conscious of making history, other than on the level of that particular time. For me the excitement came from competing with the other guys and from riding as big a wave as I was capable of riding.

Buzzy was right. I was the Pied Piper. I spent three years trying to drum up courage among all of us to surf Waimea Bay. The irony was, at the end of that first day, when we were all sitting together rehashing our rides, everybody wondered, "Why the hell have we been sitting on the beach for the past three years?" It wasn't a huge break that day. Waimea was just trying to be itself. Later we were introduced to the real Waimea.

To be Waimea, the waves have to break fifteen to eighteen feet before they start triggering on the reefs. To be good, solid Waimea, it has to be the type of break that rolls around the point, with a good, strong, twenty-foot-or-bigger swell. A lot of big-wave riders disagree on a lot of things, but I don't think any of them would disagree about this: to be good Waimea, it has to have more than size. It has to have a certain look and feel. A little bit of wind coming out of the valley, pushing the waves back, holding them up a bit.

After that first day in '57, Waimea Bay joined Sunset Beach, Noll's Reef and Laniakea as accepted North Shore surf spots. Pipeline, at that time, was still a ways down the road. All the great spots that are still the great spots today were established within our first four years in the Islands. After that, surfers surfed and named every ripple along the North Shore.

BRUCE BROWN
Surfer, Photographer, Producer of The Endless Summer

I named Velzyland when I first began making movies in '58. Velzy sponsored me and made my boards, so I named this spot on the North Shore after him. John Severson, who founded *Surfer* magazine, was also making movies at the time and named the same place, only used a different name. But Velzyland is the name that stuck. I also named Pipeline, and Severson came along and renamed it Banzai Beach. As a compromise, it became Banzai Pipeline. Now it's Pipeline again.

In the fifties, the North Shore was a dream. It was all so new. And so cheap to live there. You'd find every way you could to stretch a hundred bucks. The deal was, who could get the cheapest house and get the most people in it? You could rent a house then for sixty to seventy dollars a month. With twelve guys sharing the rent, that hundred bucks went a long way.

As Greg developed as a big-wave surfer, he'd work on all these schemes that were supposed to help a guy survive a wipeout in big surf—miniature aqualungs, tiny breathing devices. No one ever tried them out, but we all talked about it a lot. You weren't sure what would happen in an extreme situation, other than that you would most likely drown. Getting out into the lineup during big surf was a big part of the battle. No one would have thought of using a boat to get out, or a helicopter to get in.

It used to be that all the guys who rode big waves were good watermen—good swimmers, sailors or paddlers who knew the ocean, the currents and tides. You could get into a lot of trouble, get sucked to the wrong side of Waimea Bay, if you didn't know what you were doing. If you get caught in a rip at Sunset Beach you can almost do laps trying to get in. The rip runs along the beach, sucking you with it. If you know what you're doing, you can aim your board out to the break and the rip will propel you out there towards it.

At Waimea, the surf would come up fast and make real serious sounds. I remember one night when it made the windows in our house rattle. That same night, the surf covered up the telephone poles with thirty feet of sand. This tells you Waimea is closing out.

A lot of people have surfed big waves once or twice, then ended up preferring smaller waves. Greg became such a dominant big-wave rider that I can't even remember how he surfed little waves. Greg didn't analyze it, he just enjoyed it. The realization came to him later that riding big waves was good for business and helped justify his trips to the Islands each year. But even if no one had been buying boards or shooting pictures, Greg still would have been out there. The same holds true today among big-wave riders. Their enthusiasm never dies. They're eternally stoked.

Surfing won't ever die, because people get too stoked on it. I worry about the guy today who starts surfing later in life. Like a kid, this older guy wants to surf every single day. Pretty soon, he's got no wife, no kids, no job. He's living out of his car. Every surfer seems to go through those first couple of crazy, devoted years, like we did as kids, surfing every day because you never get enough of it.

Compared to other extreme sports, big-wave surfing is a neat, straightforward sport. It doesn't take much equipment to get started—a surfboard, wax, maybe a wetsuit. You get good exercise and have a lot of experiences on the ocean that you can't get anywhere else. Of course, it takes a lot of guts to go out there when the waves are breaking bigger than a house . . . That's why I stayed on shore and took pictures.

A friend of mine is a mountain climber. He looks at us surfers like we're crazy. Guys I know who are into motorcycle racing say, "Surfing! No way! Sharks could get you." Here's a guy, going a hundred and thirty miles an hour around corners who thinks that the possibility of encountering sharks is more dangerous.

I surf now for the exercise and the aesthetics. I like to see pelicans flying around and beautiful sunsets over the water. I was paddling out at a spot called Little Drake's the other day and saw a guy get a fantastic ride. It was a see-through, sun-illuminated, powder-green wave, and this guy comes squirting out of the tube. I was thrilled! The guy just brushed it off as another ride. I told him, "If that doesn't thrill you, you might as well commit suicide."

I don't think Greg Noll is aware of the legend he created. A few years ago he called me after he had taken a trip back to the North Shore. He said, "Guess what? People remember me!" I said, "Noooo shit!"

MAZATLÁN, FIRST TIME

In 1958 I went to Mazatlán. I was supposed to meet another guy down there to do some fishing and monkeying around. He never showed up. I took my skiff for fishing and decided at the last minute to also throw in my surfboard and the movie camera I had bought from Warren Miller for Australia, just in case a wave or two showed up. I had looked at the navigational charts and just couldn't see how a swell could manage to get in there, with the water protected by the tip of Baja. Of course, when I got there, I discovered that it was a great place to surf.

The Mazatlán trip turned out to be another first. The Mexicans thought surfing was pretty far-out. I found a real nice spot and made friends with one of the local boys who spoke English. He liked to watch me surf. One day I was riding a wave towards shore with the intention of coming in for the day. As I walked up onto the beach, I saw this old Mexican guy and his burro there, standing in front of me. The old man slowly backed up, making the sign of the Cross, his eyes bulging. The Mexican kid tried to calm him down.

"What's the matter with him?" I asked the kid.

"His eyesight is poor and he saw you coming across the water. He didn't realize that you were on a surfboard. He thought you were walking on water."

The poor old fart thought that his day of reckoning had come and Jesus was going to take him to his deliverance. We finally got the old man to come over and touch my board. Eventually he came back to reality and thought it was all pretty neat, riding a wave like that. I think he was more relieved than anything.

The first day I went out surfing in front of the Freeman Hotel in

Mazatlán, I didn't think anything about it. I just pulled up, took my board off the car and went down to the beach to wax up. The Chiclets kids started to gather 'round, full of curiosity. I take surfing for granted, but it's a hell of a thing for people who've never seen the sport.

The surf was three- or four-foot get-wet stuff, catch a couple of waves and goof around, have a good time. No big deal. But by the time it was over I had created a minor sensation. People came out of the hotel. A crowd of about three hundred people gathered on the beach. Every time I caught a wave or made a turn, they'd cry, "*¡Olé! ¡Olé!*" It was fun, but over the next few days it got a little tiring, so I looked for less populous places to go out.

I spent several months down there, surfing. Beverly came down and joined me. I wrote letters back to my friends—Sonny Vardeman, Rick Stoner, Reynolds Yater, Bruce Brown. "Come on down, you guys. Good surf!" On one postcard, I wrote, "The difference between Mazatlán and Hawaii is the difference between night and day. It's so beautiful down here you can't believe it. Beats the Islands to hell." I'd say anything to get them stoked so I'd have some company.

They all came down—Bruce Brown and a friend of his, Rick and Sonny, Rennie Yater and his wife. Beverly came down on a bus. We made a side trip to surf San Blas, another first. Everywhere we went we broke new ground for surfing.

I thought I would become a watermelon king and spend the rest of my life in Mexico. Invested my whole life savings—then, a hundred and fifty dollars—in watermelon seeds. The Mexicans planted them, but when the watermelons were ready to be picked, they ate them instead of picking them or harvesting them for sale.

I had an old Studebaker that was going to become my melon wagon. I went by myself to some ungodly place to fill it full of melons and ended up losing the timing gear. I was stuck there for ten days. Totally wiped me out. That was the end of my career as an agricultural baron.

Other Recollections

BEVERLY

I started out in first class on the bus from Los Angeles to San Diego. I got impatient waiting for my connection to Mexicali or wherever it was I was supposed to go next. I decided to take another bus that I was told ended up in Mazatlán, but via a different route.

I'll say. This bus took off across the desert and then just stopped in the middle of nowhere. At one stop, two *bandoleros,* guys wearing bullets across their chests and guns on their hips, got on. They didn't pay, even though everybody else had. They rode for a while, then the bus stopped and they got off in the middle of nowhere again.

I was the only gringa on the bus. Quite an experience. Something I wouldn't even consider doing now. But at age twenty it was an adventure.

Greg had a room at Señora Enrique's for about two dollars a day, including breakfast and tortillas. Señora Enrique was Spanish, but of German descent. She rented out rooms in her home. Everyone had breakfast together out on the patio. We lived there for six months, with all of our worldly possessions in the Studebaker.

One night we met a couple of guys from California in a bar. By two in the morning we were all great friends. They had just finished a race to Acapulco and were getting ready to sail back to California. They had no crew, so Greg volunteered to crew as long as they also took me. I was to do all the cooking. Neither of us knew a thing about crewing, but Greg figured we could pick it up in no time.

By six that morning, we had packed all of our possessions in the Studebaker and stored it in the police yard in Mazatlán. Then we joined our new friends on their thirty-eight-foot sailboat. We didn't know these people from the man in the moon, but away we sailed.

I was deathly ill the whole way. Couldn't even think about getting a meal off the gimbaled alcohol stove. Greg did the cooking and took turns on watch. I was green. We got as far as Cabo San Lucas, but the weather prevented us from going on around the point. In Cabo, our newfound friends decided that they needed to go home to do their income taxes. They offered us the boat for as long as we wanted to use it.

Cabo San Lucas was beautiful then. This was long before the Baja Highway was completed. There were about eight thatched huts on the beach and that was it. An oil truck came in once every two weeks by ferry from La Paz. There was plenty of food on the boat, and we fished every day.

We found an old skiff and used it to explore different, untouched beaches. The big, hundred-and-twenty-foot-long tuna seiners were all coming back up from their runs. Since the weather also prevented them from getting around the point, Cabo became one big party scene. We were invited over to different ships for dinner, to play cards. The big *Eldorado* yacht was down there. It had been Eisenhower's yacht at one time and was now a corporate yacht for Northrop Aviation. We partied on it for two or three days. A couple from England tried to sail around the point one night and ended up on the rocks. We had to rescue them.

I'll never forget that time in Cabo. Here were all these wealthy, middle-aged men attempting to have a good time and talking about the good-old days, about what a good time they used to have, instead of dealing with today. That really registered, left an impression with me that you've got to make every day really count. You don't want to end up down the road, looking back and saying, "Gee, remember the good ol' days . . . "

Greg and I had an extremely interesting life together. It seems we lived ten lifetimes in the time we were together. I look at other married couples and I realize that we did anything and everything that came along. There was always a new adventure in the works. I would never have embarked on half the things we did without Greg. Greg always made everything O.K. If he was there it was O.K.

We built empires, tore them down and rebuilt them, then tore them down again. We fell down the big ladder so many times that it became no big deal. We'd just get up, brush ourselves off and say, "Here we go again."

Other Recollections

BRUCE BROWN

I remember that trip to Mazatlán very well because I had a '50 Kaiser and Greg had a '47 Studebaker. My buddies and I caravaned down there and met Greg. He was making his first surf movie. At that time I hadn't even started making movies.

Greg's Studebaker broke down in a melon field during one of our excursions. He found some Mexican guy who had a hammer and chisel and was willing to work on it. It looked to us like Greg was going to be stuck there for a few days, so we drove on with plans to meet him later.

The big deal then was to be the one to name a new surf spot. Greg was real pissed because we got there first and named Cannon's Point, among others that we ran into between Mazatlán and San Blas. Greg liked to name them himself.

———————————

MAKING MOVIES

BUFFALO KEAULANA

Greg tell me, "Go to movies with me. We in movies. I take you." So I go. Movie come on. See me and Greg on wave. "Dere me!" I shout. Me pau. "Dere Greg!" I shout. Next wave, "Dere Greg!" And next wave, dere Greg. Next wave, dere Greg, dere Greg, dere Greg. I no go to movies afta dat.

On my way back from Australia, I stayed over in the Islands for a few weeks. Beverly joined me there and we took more movies of different North Shore surf spots. I made my first surf film from that trip. I showed it in high school auditoriums, charged a buck to get in and pocketed the money. The county lifeguards gave me all kinds of static for going down there on their money and making a film.

We had a lot of interesting adventures, surfing and making movies. Once, on the island of Molokai, I asked this young Hawaiian kid who had grown up there how I'd go about getting a pass onto Cook's Ranch. Cook's Ranch was made up of old missionary land and it's all restricted area.

The kid said, "I've lived here all my life and I've never been in there. You can't get in there."

I decided to go into the office at the ranch and explain to them what I was doing. I put on my most responsible look and told them we wanted to make a little surf film and that we'd be good guys and not mess up the property. We just wanted to do a little surf travelog. The guy went and talked to somebody and came back with the key to the gate.

We found a neat little surf spot there, but it was the ranch itself that was really interesting. As we drove through the grounds, we saw antelope and zebra and all sorts of exotic animals that had been turned loose out there. This kid who was with us couldn't believe we had actually got in. We took movies of the whole thing and slipped it in among the surf scenes. It added a special touch to the movie.

Other Recollections

SONNY VARDEMAN

Greg did the same thing with Warren Miller as he did with Dale Velzy. Greg got interested in making movies and hounded Miller to death, asking how he made these damn films, what kind of equipment did he use, how did the camera work?

Bruce Brown actually became interested in making movies after watching Greg do his stuff in Mazatlán. John Severson also got into movie-making for a while. But the pioneer of the surf movie was Bud Browne. Bud was a lifeguard with us, too. For years, surfers would come from up and down the coast to congregate in Santa Monica a couple times a year to see Bud Browne's latest surf movie. You'd see all the people you'd met that year at different surf spots along the coast.

The turnout was tremendous. People cheering in the aisles, hooting and howling. Greg sees the light and decides to make his own surf films.

Greg took films in Australia when he was there for the paddling contests, and also in Hawaii. When he went to Mazatlán in '58, that turned out to be another movie. The title and format of each movie became *Search for Surf*. Every year became a sequel to the previous year.

When Greg told me and Rick Stoner about the surf in Mazatlán, we hitched up a teardrop trailer to my '47 Ford, strapped our surfboards on top and took off to join him. We spent nearly three months down there, traveling up and down the coast from Mazatlán, with Greg taking pictures. We went as far south as San Blas and Zihuatanejo. We had to go inland through Guadalajara and then back out to the coast to get there.

Mexico turned out not to be a big-wave spot. There were a few days of twelve-to-fifteen-foot waves, way outside. These were very rare, though. Most of the time the surf was small, two to four feet.

When we came home, we all helped Greg edit his film. Greg designed his narration after Warren Miller's, which was done live. Greg rented the Pier Avenue Auditorium, which became the mecca of surf films for a while. Rick Stoner, Mike Stange, other friends and I helped pass out fliers, sell tickets, usher people.

I mean to say, that first *Search for Surf* from the Australian and Mazatlán trips created a mob scene. The auditorium held three hundred people, but there were at least four hundred. The aisles were packed and the fire marshall was having a fit. Greg cranked up the Hawaiian music, got the film rolling and everyone quieted down to watch and listen. It was a hype job and it worked. He'd run the movie two or three nights in a row. Charged a buck a person and filled the auditorium to overflowing every night.

One night, people were lined up around the block, waiting to get in. I went outside and sold tickets to people who had exact change. My pockets were full of dollar bills. We had no idea how many tickets we were selling. The fire marshall would come and raise holy hell, threaten to close the place down.

From the proceeds of that movie, Greg bought himself a new Volkswagen van. He was the talk of the town in his new van.

A year or two later, Greg rented the Santa Monica Civic Auditorium, which held about five thousand people. We had a pressure-packed, raucous crowd the first night. Greg had the music going before the film started. People got even more worked up. Prior to the film, Greg would usually go up on stage, introduce himself and tell a little about where the film was taken. This evening, the crowd was just going crazy, and Greg was up on stage, getting pelted by beer and soft drink caps. He finally retreated and turned on the film and, again, everyone settled down at once.

Greg made surf movies for six or seven years. When he got into the big time with his surfboard factory, he stopped making movies and devoted all his time to the business.

BEVERLY

I remember many times, lying in bed in the middle of the night, listening to the surf building at Waimea. I knew Greg heard it, too, but I never said anything. It wasn't a time to say anything. We would get up at the break of day and drive to Waimea Bay. We'd look and sometimes we'd make several dry runs, but there was never any conversation. The tension coming off Greg was extreme. He would ask me, "Do you have the cameras? Do you have extra film?"

When it was time, we'd get situated. I'd always go out on the point, next to Bud Browne. Bud would have his cameras there and I would have mine and we'd shoot film all day. I ran both the movie camera and the still camera. Greg always took the time to get me set up. Then he'd go back and get his board and it was like another person who would walk back by, on his way to the water. Everyone on the beach would ooh and aah. The crowd was always there and I had all this confidence in this man.

I knew that when he went out in the water that morning, it was going to be near dark before he came back in. Everyone else would be coming and going and Greg would sit out there. He would surf all day and never come out of the water. I watched him go under a couple of times on big wipeouts and I wondered if he was ever coming up. I would get nervous, pace a little. But Greg told me to never take my eye out of that camera, so, as nervous as I might have been, I was still ready to film whatever happened. I knew I'd get my butt chewed if I missed anything.

The first time I joined Greg in Hawaii was when he came back from Australia. We lived in a van, cruised around to the different surf spots and camped out. We often camped out wherever we went and in whatever vehicle we had at the time. When we showed films, we traveled up and down the California coast and always slept in the back of our vehicle or crashed at somebody's house. I'd sit for hours with Greg, going over his dialogue with him. Or I'd time him while he held his breath for two-and-a-half and three-minute stretches. He'd practice for hours.

BRUCE BROWN

Greg's surf films were just as good or better as anyone else's at that time. Beverly took a lot of the movies and stills while Greg was out surfing.

When we were in Hawaii one winter, and both of us were making movies, I asked Greg what f-stop he was using. Greg said, "What's that?"

"You know, the lens setting."

"I don't know," Greg said. "The guy at the store where I bought the camera set it up for me and I just left it there."

As a photographer, I'd feel a little reluctant to pump up a guy to go out in big waves at places like Waimea, Pipeline or Kaena Point, just so I could photograph him. What if he ended up maimed or killed? Since Greg's movies often starred himself at these places, it was a perfect setup for him.

I remember the time Greg came in at the end of the day with the first footage of Waimea Bay. We all gathered together at the Seaview Inn in Haleiwa and watched it, frame by frame, on Greg's portable viewer. One sequence featured Mike Stange free-falling down the face of a gigantic wave. It was unbelievable to look at, but Greg thought it was great. He kept pounding Mike on the back, saying, "Unbelievable! Shit, Mike, how'd ya feel after that?"

In 1965, the year after I released *The Endless Summer*, Greg stopped making movies to concentrate on his surfboard business. That's when he built his fabulous surfboard factory on a dump site in Hermosa Beach.

The Endless Summer was my last movie. I had made about six by then. People used to tell me, "Now that you're making movies, you ought to move to Hollywood." I'd say, "Bullshit." Like many other surfers, I'd found something I was good at, something that earned me enough money to keep surfing.

As kids, none of us would ever have imagined that we could make money surfing. Our goal was to find some way to make money so we could go surfing. Like Greg, many of us were able to make a business out of what we loved doing. And although there was an air of competitiveness among us, we also admired each other. There was no jealousy.

Other Recollections

LEROY GRANNIS
Surfer and Surf Photographer

You knew you were going to get some action whenever Greg went in the water. He pushed himself. He'd get as far back in the wave as possible. Maybe too far. He liked being on the edge.

Greg and José Angel were alike in the way they approached riding big waves. They blew each other's minds and the minds of the spectators on shore.

I became a surf photographer in 1958. I had developed an ulcer and was told by my doctor to find an occupation less stressful that the one I was in. I'd been surfing in Southern California since the thirties, so the photography angle seemed a natural extension for me.

I was down at the Manhattan Beach Pier in the early sixties, fooling around with a new camera that had a big, three-hundred-sixty-millimeter lens. Greg happened to be out surfing that day. The backwash hit the wave he was on and bounced Greg off his board and into the air, level with the top of the pier. It was a fantastic image and I had him in the viewfinder, but by the time the shutter went off, Greg had disappeared. That's when I learned that a slow camera was going to be no good for surf photography.

Surfing's popularity also spawned a series of Hollywood surf movies in the late fifties and early sixties. Movies such as *Beach Blanket Bingo, Gidget* and *Ride the Wild Surf* gave teenagers everywhere a glimpse of Hollywood's version of the surf culture.

Movie companies hired real surfers such as Mickey Dora, Phil Edwards, Mike Doyle, Mickey Muñoz and me to do the stunt work for different actors, including Frankie Avalon, Fabian and Jimmy Darren.

Being the smallest of the bunch, Muñoz was hired to do stunt work for whichever actress was currently playing Gidget.

For the authentic wave-riding scenes in *Ride the Wild Surf,* the film company came to the North Shore. It happened to be one of Waimea's bigger weeks. I hadn't been hired to stunt for this movie, but I was out there surfing and ended up getting in the way in so much of the footage that the producers decided to change the movie to conform to the actual surfing. They hired another actor, Jim Mitchum, and wrote him into the script. They made him some black-and-white striped trunks like mine, and I earned stunt pay.

When John Milius released *Big Wednesday* in 1978, his company found a picture that had been taken of me in 1964, standing on the beach at Pipeline, holding my board and wearing the striped trunks. For the movie's promotional poster, they superimposed two guys sitting on the sand next to me. In reality, that picture was taken the day Mike Stange and I surfed Outside Pipeline. I was watching the shorebreak, which is the wave you see in the picture, and trying to decide on the best way to get to the outside break.

When the studio was ready to release the poster, they suddenly discovered that they didn't have a release on the picture. They called me and asked if I would sign one. I agreed, and they flew a gal up here to Crescent City to get my signature and give me a check.

In 1956, following my trip to Australia and the release of my surf movie, I was invited to appear on Bill Burrud's "Assignment America" TV show to show part of the movie. Tom Malone, who also had a TV show, caught Burrud's show and invited me to appear on his program. Malone used my surfing footage pretty regularly for a few years, and he and I eventually became buddies. But at first the guy nearly drove me nuts.

Burrud's show had been very professionally done. Malone's show, which covered a lot of different sports, seemed to always be thrown together at the last minute. Malone was a little scattered. He always was getting himself in a jam with his programming. He'd call me at the last minute and ask, "Could you bring me fifteen minutes of surf film?"

I didn't know anything about television. I just followed directions. On the first show I did for Malone, just as they began rolling my film and I started my narration, Malone signals to me that he's got to go fetch some papers. I continue my narration. The film ends. They run a commercial and Malone is still gone. This is live TV, so the crew starts motioning for me to begin talking. For a very long minute or two, I'm going on about surfing and what we're going to show in the next segment, blah, blah, blah—I have no idea what I said—and Malone finally comes rushing in to bail me out. I was never so frightened in my life. All those cameras and lights staring down your throat.

As surfing became more popular, Malone's ratings went up. He started bringing in live audiences of twenty to thirty kids for the surf shows. I'd show a film, then Malone would open it up for people watching at home to call in with a surf question for Greg Noll. Malone would first take the call, in case he had to censor anything, then he'd pass along the question to me. Kids would ask questions like "Would you ask Greg Noll to explain the expression 'hang ten'?" Or "What does 'cowabunga' mean?"

On one particular show, we'd gone through several questions before Malone announced that he'd take one last call. Malone was in one of his distracted moods, so the question goes right by him. He turns to me and says, "We have a caller who wants to know what the surfing term 'beat off' means."

Right there on the air. The kids in the audience rolled in the aisles, hooting and laughing, and Malone gets red in the face. As soon as the words had left his mouth, he tried to stuff them back in. I say, as calmly as possible, "Gee, Tom, that's a new one on me."

For the next month, everywhere I went, I got razzed about the new surfing term, "beat off."

After becoming established as a surfboard manufacturer and surf film producer whose films were shown on TV, all of a sudden all the teachers and counselors who wanted nothing to do with my ass during school were wanting to kiss it. They'd be interviewed by a newspaper or magazine and their tone would change. "Oh yes, I knew Greg Noll. He was in my class. Fine, upstanding young man." What bullshit.

EVOLUTION OF THE
MODERN SURFBOARD

Mike Stange and I got into surfing at the absolute perfect time, during the last glimmer of the redwood/balsa days. In many of the photographs from that era, you see redwood and balsa boards side-by-side. When I first started surfing, Bob Simmons was just beginning to experiment with other materials. You'd hear a few stories about new, revolutionary Simmons boards, but up to that time there was Matt Kivlin and Joe Quigg riding redwoods at Malibu. Doc Ball and the guys at the Palos Verdes Surfboard Club. Velzy, Leroy Grannis, Ted Kerwin, the Edgar Brothers at Hermosa and Manhattan. Lorrin Harrison, Burrhead and the guys at San Onofre. A few guys down in La Jolla. The entire surfing population consisted of maybe a couple hundred guys, most of them riding redwood boards, paddleboards and balsa/redwoods.

Then along came the gremmies—me, Bing Copeland and Buzzy Bent—watching these guys stick those long redwood boards in the shorebreak and pearl on them. There was no scoop on the nose of those boards, and they were so heavy that one arm became longer than the other when you carried them down to the water. Still, surfing looked like a neat thing to do, once you mastered it.

You hear about those of us who began surfing during that era as the "pioneers of modern surfing," but I don't think any of us had any sense of history about what we were doing. We were having fun. It does intrigue me that our era produced so many distinct individuals. I don't see that happening as much today. Maybe it's because there's just too many people and the whole thing gets lost. Surfing still allows you to become your own person, as long as you don't let the hype get in your way. The sport itself hasn't changed, but for some people, the reason for doing it has changed.

Once Bob Simmons got into surfing, his engineering background surfaced and he immediately started working on better ways to build boards. His boards were an instant success. He experimented with different materials, such as sandwiching balsa, plywood and Styrofoam together to try to get the weight down. Equally as important as his use of lighter materials was his use of fiberglass. He was the first to combine light weight and fiberglass, and this blew the whole thing wide open.

Simmons always paddled on his knees. With his ginked-up arm he had one good dig on one side and a little scratch on the other. His boards were wide because of his handicap. His style of surfing was to just slide across the face of the wave without much maneuvering.

Kivlin and Quigg did some shaping in Simmons' shop. They took the same principles Simmons used and applied them to balsa wood and to the needs of the average surfer. That's how the Malibu board evolved. Velzy came in behind them. I was behind Velzy by about three years.

During that time, surfboards went through some rapid design changes. Within a three-to-four-year period, we're talking about going from redwoods to the Simmons-type board to the Malibu board. The Malibu board was a lightweight, balsa board designed off the Simmons theory of reducing the weight, but it also went one step further by improving the shape and thus the maneuverability of the board.

At one time, Simmons' boards were in such demand that the pressure of meeting orders almost became too much for him. Like most of us, he really just wanted to surf. I remember once, he had something like thirty-four boards on back-order. Velzy and I both had had a Simmons board on back-order for three months. Simmons wouldn't answer his phone, so Velzy decided that we would check out the situation in person.

Going to Simmons' shop was just as much an experience as riding one of his boards. The shop was on a side street in Venice Beach. It was an absolute goddamn mess. He never cleaned up the balsa-wood shavings, so you'd have to make a path through the shavings and other debris to get from one place in the shop to another.

Velzy and I arrived there about five o'clock one afternoon. The place looked all shut down. We pounded on the door. No reply. Velzy noticed that the door wasn't locked, so he opened it and called, "Simmons?"

No reply. We walked in cautiously through the shavings, calling, "Simmons, where are you?" Finally, we heard a gruff voice from a corner: "Whaddaya want." We followed the voice and found Simmons sitting in the corner in shadow. He was eating beans out of a can, using a big balsa-wood shaving for a spoon.

Simmons was eccentric. When he'd worn holes through the soles of his shoes, he'd cut out a piece of plywood and tape it onto his shoe. With his perpetually uncombed hair, skinny physique and gimpy arm, he truly looked like a mad scientist.

He didn't like many people, but he liked Velzy better than most because Velzy rode Simmons' boards and he rode them well. Besides that, he just liked Velzy. Simmons was upset that Kivlin and Quigg were adapting his board design to the quicker, more maneuverable Malibu style. I remember him saying, "That's not what you want to do." I later realized that he was building boards for himself. He thought that everyone should ride the way he did.

Even so, Simmons' major contribution to surfing was the transition to lighter-weight boards and the use of fiberglass. He provided the link between the redwood board and the modern surfboard. It would have happened eventually, but without Simmons coming along at that time, board design might have gone through another ten years of stagnation. Simmons has earned himself a niche in surfing history, but very few surfers have ever heard of him.

Simmons was a loner. He had a habit of going off by himself to surf. He hated any type of crowd. He liked Salt Creek, below Laguna Beach. It wasn't unusual to go there and find Simmons, by himself. Or someplace else, like Tijuana Sloughs. Places that the usual surfing crowd didn't go.

He spent about a year on the North Shore, lived at Sunset Beach when everyone else was oriented to Makaha. I remember Buzzy Trent saying that he'd drive by Sunset and see Simmons sitting out there by himself. The story got around that, whenever you went to a surf spot, expecting to have the place to yourself, Simmons would already be there. Even if it was a stormy, rainy day, you'd see Simmons, sitting out in the water by himself.

One day, I ditched school and talked Simmons into taking me with him to Salt Creek. He didn't like kids any more than he liked adults, but I also rode one of his boards, so he tolerated me. He'd go through long periods of silence, then he'd start quizzing me. "Why are you going to school? What are you going to do with your education? Why don't you get out and do something with your life?" He was provocative and he was smart. A real individual.

Bob Simmons was killed at Windansea, in San Diego, in 1954. Got slapped on the head by his own board and that was it. The irony of it is that it was only a six-or eight-foot day. That's the way it always goes. For the most part, it's not the big waves that get a guy. It's always some quirky thing.

One of the reasons that Kivlin and Quigg were so successful with the Malibu board is that they had the perfect testing ground. The Malibu wave is like a made-to-order perfect tube. They could test their designs on these uncrowded, machinelike waves, then come in and make improvements. During that short period of a few years, surfboard design made a leap like going from horse and buggy to motorcars.

For years, balsa-wood boards were the thing. In the early fifties, Velzy joined up with another surfer named Hap Jacobs to make boards under the label Velzy and Jacobs. I was fifteen and making my own boards. Hobie Alter was starting to make boards in Dana Point. Larry Gordon's and Floyd Smith's operation, Gordon and Smith, popped up in San Diego. Dewey Weber worked for Velzy before going out on his own. Other guys, including Rick Stoner, Bing Copeland, Mike Bright and Sonny Vardeman, also went into business, and the whole surfboard industry exploded. There were a lot of guys up and down the coast by then who were making their own boards in their backyards, but those that I've named were among those who actually set up shop.

What really was important about the transition from redwood to balsa was that it caused all hell to break loose. Now surfing styles began to evolve along with equipment changes. Suddenly there was a board you could actually surf. You didn't have to spend all your time trying to keep the board from pearling and picking sand crabs out of your ears. And, it didn't take you all summer to learn to catch a wave. The balsa board allowed more people to get into surfing. To really appreciate the evolution of the modern surfboard, every surfer today ought to take out a redwood board and try to catch a wave on the goddamn thing.

In the late fifties, Hobie and Grubby Clark started experimenting with foam. I think some of Hobie's first designs in foam were racing boards. Soon the word on this new material started spreading up and down the coast.

Foam didn't change surfboard design that much. The weight was pretty much on par with balsa wood. What foam did was stabilize and streamline design. You could make the same type of board, over and over again, without worrying about different weights of wood, bad grain and such.

With balsa wood, you had to depend on getting quality wood. As balsa boards grew in popularity, there was a real competition among us shapers to get the best balsa. In the early fifties, the best source was General Veneer in South Gate. I happened to live close to the factory, so anytime a new shipment came in I was right on top of it. It was a mad scramble to go through every piece of wood and select the lightest and highest-quality wood. The weight and quality of every surfboard depended upon what type of wood arrived on each shipment at General Veneer from South America. Once foam caught on, that concern was eliminated. You could control the density of the foam. It was an important step forward.

Before he sold the foam blank operation to Clark, Hobie had his foam blanks all to himself. In the meantime, Harold Walker also had started making foam blanks and was selling them to Gordon Duane, who had opened the first surf shop in Huntington Beach that year, in '59. Gordie had gotten interested in surfing in the early fifties when he was in the navy and stationed in Hawaii. He had been making balsa boards since then, but now was beginning the transition to foam boards.

I had just come in from surfing at the Huntington Beach Pier one day when I saw this truck go by, loaded with foam blanks. Like a spy, I followed it to Gordie's shop. When the truck driver was done unloading the blanks, I confronted him. "Hey, where are these things coming from? What's the deal here?" He told me to follow him back to the factory. I did, and I worked out a deal with Harold Walker. Harold and I went on to become good friends and spent some memorable times in the Islands together.

I soon became the third guy on the coast to use foam. Eventually, my father, Ash Noll, who was a chemist, figured out a formula and helped me devise a way to mold my own foam. The way we did this is an all-time story in itself. One afternoon, my dad and I went over to Grubby's house just to visit. Along with a few ulterior motives, I also brought along a case of beer. Grubby ended up drinking one too many and started talking about his formula. My dad, being an astute individual and chemist, calmly took in every word while I encouraged Grubby's rambling. Grubby woke up the next morning with a hangover and I woke up with a foam formula.

It wasn't long before Velzy and Jacobs also started using Walker foam. I think Dewey Weber used it, too. When Grubby Clark made Clark Foam available industry-wide, the whole thing blew wide open. Every board shaper started using foam blanks and the balsa board faded into oblivion.

I'll never forget cutting into my first foam blank. It smelled so strange. Balsa wood has a good smell to it. Foam dust didn't have the soft feel of balsa dust, either. Foam dust was raspy, scratchy. Made you want to wash up all the time. Working with balsa wood was more like an art form, and there aren't many guys today who are capable of doing it. It was sad to see an end to the balsa-wood era.

Other Recollections

GORDON "GRUBBY" CLARK
Surfer, Founder of Clark Foam, world's largest supplier of foam cores for surfboards

I was working for Hobie as a glasser when he decided to devote one hundred percent of his efforts to developing foam boards. You have to know Hobie to be able to understand what this meant. When he decides to do something, he goes into it one hundred percent. In January '58, Hobie threw out all his balsa-wood stuff and said, "This is the way it's going to be. Foam."

Two years before, Dave Sweet and his brother, both surfers with a shop in Santa Monica, had found a backer in the actor Cliff Robertson, who had starred with Sandra Dee in the first Gidget film. Robertson financed their work in developing a polyurethane foam surfboard. In 1950, Bob Simmons had been the very first to ever try foam in a surfboard—he used polystyrene foam. Many others have claimed to have been the first to try polyurethane foam, but Lorrin Harrison in Capistrano Beach was actually the first, in 1955. The work started by Sweet in 1956 was the first sustained effort in developing polyurethane foam boards.

Hobie came out with his first polyurethane foam boards in June of '58, followed by Sweet. Sweet had figured out the foam before then, but he had had trouble building a board design that worked. Everyone takes foam boards for granted now, but in those days it was quite a challenge to figure out the glassing, how to use fill coating or hot coating. We all went through a lot of broken boards during that time.

As soon as his foam boards were available, Hobie became hopelessly backlogged. There was a lot of competition coming on then, but Hobie and Sweet weren't about to sell foam blanks to a third party. This opened up an opportunity for another team, Chuck Foss and Harold Walker. Foss was the resin expert; Walker made the foam blanks.

In '61, Hobie's original tooling had become too slow to compete with a full-time foam-blank manufacturer who could run several shifts and grind out blanks one after another. We knew it was time to build new molds and new designs, but it didn't make sense to do it all for just one surfboard shop. So I bought the few tools that could still be used, formed Clark Foam and started working on new molds and new processes right away.

Clark got his nickname when he was going to Pomona College, studying physics and math. He lived out of a battered old pickup truck that he used for weekend surf trips. Both he and his pickup had a grubby look. In the mid-sixties, Grubby and I went 'round and 'round for about three years over a bill. I owed him about three hundred dollars for some blanks and we got into an argument about how it was to be paid. We bounced that bill back and forth until it finally became kind of a fun deal.

Grubby kept sending this guy named George Draper, who worked for him, to my shop to try to collect the money. Whenever Draper was making the rounds, delivering foam blanks to other surf shops in the area—in Hermosa Beach alone, there were about ten of us within a ten-block stretch—he'd stop by my shop for the money.

I'd take him out for a drink. He'd get drunk and end up going off on his own, sometimes not showing up back at work for a couple of days. Nobody would be getting foam blanks, and Grubby would be pounding his desk: "Damn that Greg Noll, he owes me three hundred bucks and now he's turning my deliveryman into a drunk!"

One night, I had Draper out drinking with me and we got shit-faced. I wrote out a check to Grubby for forty thousand dollars and signed it Donald Duck. Grubby took that check to every bank in Southern California, trying to get it cashed. He came close once, and the bank called me to see if I was really Donald Duck. I was sweating it! He'd have cleaned me out.

In our hell-raising, Grubby and I had some pretty good times together. It didn't take too many beers for Grubby to get rolling. And, once he got rolling with the foam-blank business, it didn't take too many years before he was the king of the hill. Grubby doesn't need my three hundred bucks now.

The first actual shortboards came up from Australia in the late sixties. They were taken over to the Islands, where they caused a sensation. Charlie Galanto, a big-wave surfer who had opened a Greg Noll Surfboards shop in Honolulu, got excited and hopped a plane to California to see me. "Greg, it's coming!" he said. We designed a shortboard just under eight feet in length and called it the Bug Board. Charlie took a bunch of them back to his shop.

At one point, we had a couple hundred of these new shortboards on racks in one of the back rooms. Don Hansen, who still owns a surf shop in Encinitas, walked into our factory one day and happened to see all these shortboards. "What the hell is going on, Greg?" he said. "Am I missing out on something?" Within months, everyone had figured it out and the shortboard boom was on.

Both Dewey and I messed around with shortboard designs, but we turned them out in the longer, traditional style. I never really saw the full potential of the shortboard as it has become today. The Australians deserve the credit for designing the true shortboard and for causing the shortboard revolution.

News story from Honolulu Star-Bulletin, Friday, December 5, 1969, following day at Big Makaha.

'A Life or Death Situation'
Storm Wave Wipes Out Champ Surfer

By Tomi Knaefler
Star-Bulletin Writer

Greg Noll, one of the best of the big wave riders, yesterday came uncomfortably close to being a victim of Oahu's surf storm.

Noll and six other big league surfers were drawn to the challenge of the massive 25-foot waves at Makaha.

About 1:30 p.m., Noll chose his challenge which another surfing champ, Fred Hemmings, described as "the biggest wave I've ever seen ridden."

BUT THE RIDE came to an abrupt and terrifying halt only moments after it began. Noll was "wiped out and there I was straight under

the wave and all I could see was a tiny patch of sunlight." Then he was tossed like a toothpick in the turbulent sea.

ing a "giant Wall of China falling on you."

Noll was carried down in a rip tide, then battled swiftly moving currents a...

weren't riding the waves.

Froiseth, who had chaired the Makaha international surfing contests or mary

was the "nastiest" Makaha has ever been.

ONE OBS...

So it was, even down along the coast Nanakuli.

iv predicta...

'BUSTED BOARD'—Surf champ Greg Noll goes through the ritual of washing off his board, however "finished" he says it is following a terrifying "wipe out" while riding a gigantic 25-foot wave at Makaha yesterday.—Photo by Albert Yamauchi.

---

fred hemmings jr.
2909 KALAKAUA AVE.   HONOLULU, HAWAII 96815

February 1,1970

Mr. Greg Noll
717 Valley Drive
Hermosa Beach, California

Dear Greg,

        I persoally believe the waves at Makaha that famous day were the largest I have ever been in. Also the wave you took off on was the most massive wall of water I have ever seen anyone attempt to ride. With todays publicity centering around goons sailing psycodelically around in the world of small wave performance, I feel that there are only a few surfers who can say they can also ride mountains of water that can swallow a surfer up FOREVER. This is a special feeling that most of the surfing populus will never even concieve of in their wildest dreams. So, I'd say we are getting something very exclusive on those rare days of huge Makaha surf. We were lucky to be there.

ALOHA, BRA

frederick

Letter from Fred Hemmings, written after Big Makaha in '69.

Greg and his mother, Gracie, 1938.

Greg at Palos Verdes Cove, 1950.

Greg scooping bait off the bait boat, Manhattan Beach Pier, 1948. Greg's house can be seen above the three men on the pier.

Monkeying around at San Onofre. From left: Bing Copeland, Tubesteak Tracy, Greg and Mickey Dora. 1951.

Dale Velzy and Hap Jacobs show an early balsa-wood twin-fin design. Early fifties.

Mike Stange, Steve Voorhees, Greg and Billy Ming at Makaha, 1955.

Trophy winners in 1951 Santa Monica paddleboard race, standing in front of Bev Morgan's Chevy. From left: Bing Copeland, Bev Morgan, Greg Noll, Dick Medvie, Bob Hogan.

Thirty-two-mile Catalina-to-Manhattan Beach Rough Water Paddleboard Race, 1955. From left: Charlie Reimers, Greg Noll, Tommy Zahn, Ricky Grigg (first place), George Downing, Bob Hogan.

Beverly on the beach
at Mazatlán, 1958.

Making movies in Mazatlán, 1958.

The Greg Noll Surf Team prepares
to leave the Hermosa Beach shop for
an East Coast tour in 1964. From left:
John Leinao, Gene Brown, Cully
Ragland and Bobby Dallas.

Laura, about 1961.

Early ad and price list, about 1963.

GREG NOLL
SURF BOARDS and FILM PRODUCTIONS

1402 Pacific Coast Hwy. • Hermosa Beach, California • FR 6-4898

UP to 8'6"	$100.00		9'7" to 10'	$115.00
8'7" to 9'	105.00		10'1" to 10'6"	125.00
9'1" to 9'6"	110.00		10'7" to 11'	130.00

GUN SHAPES............*Semi $10.00 extra...........*Full $140.00

Trade-ins are valued according to their condition

- Four pound density foam guaranteed not to expand or turn yellow under normal conditions
- Two layers of 10 ounce cloth
- Double overlapped rails
- Round or square glass fin
- ¾" redwood strip
- Clear finish
- Every surfboard is custom shaped and fiberglassed in our fully equipped shop to your individual requirements.

EXTRAS:

Balsa or Redwood Strips
½" $3.00
1½" 5.00
2½" 8.00
* Special strip designs and colors quoted on request.

ALSO AVAILABLE:

- New custom boards in stock
- Used boards all sizes
- We specialize in repair work
- Full stock of fiberglass supplies and surfing accessories
- Surf Films also available on request
- Tax will be added to above prices.

ROUGH GUIDE FOR CORRECT BOARD SIZES

Under 100 lbs.	8'2"	Under 175 lbs.	9'8"
Under 125 lbs.	8'8"	Under 200 lbs.	10'2"
Under 150 lbs.	9'2"	Under 225 lbs.	10'8"

Greg (left) and Mike Stange in a dual wipeout at Waimea Bay, early sixties. Half the nose of Mike's board was missing.

In 1964, this was hailed as ''The Biggest Wave Ever Ridden.'' Greg Noll, Waimea Bay.

Greg Noll at Sunset Beach in the mid-sixties.

Greg Noll, Outside Pipeline takeoff, November 1964. The wave grew from twenty feet at takeoff to twenty-five feet.

Mickey Dora and Greg, during the filming of *Ride the Wild Surf*. Waimea Bay, mid-sixties.

da CATS' Theory of Evolution

RETARDESS KOOKUS

The earliest stage, unworthy of discussion.

PIGMIO PHAINAS

Characterized by small structure and jerky, uncoordinated movements, little ability.

MALIBUIS MASOCHSCUS

Recognized by determined expression on face, but no ability. This short structured musclehead resorts to throwing of objects and threats abortive attempts to make waves.

VALLEI SAN FERNANDO

This small-brained inland migrant is only mentioned because of the peculiar habits they have of traveling in packs and futile attempts to look skilled on waves over one foot. It is hoped that they will soon become extinct.

HOMO COOPERI

The first stage with any skill. This form was unable to move in a limited way . . . however, this form was unable to compete with the earlier forms and became extinct.

I have been asked by several leading Universities to clarify the various stages of evolution in the history of surfing. Much time and research has gone into these studies and the final results. *Mickey Dora*

Mickey Dora 🐾 da CAT

MAFIAS DANA POINTIS

This form will survive only as long as its food supply lasts. This being the earlier stage of evolution with their dull wit and idle worship. This form is easily recognized by its pleasant smile and gaudy outfits. It is quick to sell out to any side.

DECENTUS INDIVIDUALIST

Easily recognized once it is spotted. Although this is a very rare form it is serious and intelligent in its action. He possesses skill and cunning, and his type probably led to the final stage.

HOMOSAPENS MICKEY DORA

The peak of perfection has all the qualities of the latter stage plus more advanced knowledge and ability. Uses only one model . . . da Cat . . . a very rare form, the only one known.

One of the most famous, or infamous, ads in da Cat series, "da Cat's Theory of Evolution."

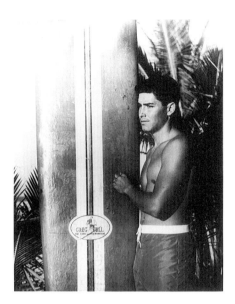

José Angel, 1965.

Peter Cole, 1965.

Greg and Henry Preece, mid-sixties.

Buffalo Keaulana and Greg, mid-sixties.

Finishers in the 1967 Duke Kahanamoku Invitational, from left: Ricky Grigg (first place), Fred Hemmings (third), Felipe Pomar (fourth) and Greg Noll (eighth). All rode Greg Noll surfboards.

Duke Kahanamoku and Greg at the Duke Invitational award ceremonies.

Greg, Violet Trent, Buzzy Trent and Flippy Hoffman, 1965.

Sonny Vardeman, 1982.

Greg on the *Ashlyne,* 1981.

Greg and Mike Stange fishing in
Crescent City, 1988.

Ken Bradshaw and Greg, 1988.

The wall at Malibu, 1988.

PRANKSTERS

One day in December '58 a friend, Bob Sheppard, let me borrow a pair of his trunks while we were surfing at Haleiwa. I got hit by a board and broke two ribs. Buffalo had to bring me in. At first, Buff thought I was kidding. The board knocked the air out of me, and all I could do was say, in a little squeaky voice, "Buff, help me." He finally came over to see what was wrong and paddled me in.

They took me to the hospital. Sheppard was there, tugging at my trunks. "Give 'em to me, you bastard, before you croak." I got my ribs taped up and decided to fly home that night, since the broken ribs ended my winter season.

About three months went by, then I get this letter from Sheppard: "On December 14, 1958, you willfully and without permission, removed and donned one pair of blue trunks from Robert Sheppard's car. You were unfortunately the victim of a slight accident while surfing that day and while being treated for the acquired injury, you undoubtedly saved much money as the doctor had at one time been an Outrigger Canoe Club member. Not wishing to inconvenience you more, you were allowed to keep the trunks only with the understanding that they would be left with Paul Swanson upon your departure to the Mainland. I have now been informed that you have ungratefully skipped out without returning those irreplaceable and highly valuable trunks. I am bringing this to your attention and I am sure you will immediately airmail the trunks to the above address, you kook."

I ignored the letter and wore the trunks for about five more months, until they were just a pile of threads. Then I wrapped what was left of them with some bricks and put them in a box. Sent them airmail special delivery, C.O.D., to Sheppard in Hawaii. Probably cost him about $25.

I'm sure that before he opened the package, Sheppard thought, "Well, Greg is going to be good-hearted and send me something really bitchin' for the use of my trunks."

We usually threw a shop party on the day of Christmas Eve. One winter, just before I was scheduled to leave for my annual trip to the Islands, people were getting out of their jobs early and stopping by the shop for a little Christmas cheer. Kit Horn came by to see if I would be available to go to Lunada Bay in the next couple of days. Lunada Bay is off the Palos Verdes Peninsula and breaks only on a big winter swell. It's a big, steep wave with a fast takeoff. Under the right swell conditions, the place could become very hairy. In 1963, we got several days over fifteen feet. The bay was rock-rimmed and enclosed by a hundred-and-fifty-foot cliff from point to point, with only one small trail down to the water.

Not many people have heard of Kit Horn. He was a good friend and schoolmate of Buzzy Trent's. And a frustrated big-wave rider. If you had asked the guy what he wanted to be when he grew up, he would have said that he wanted to go to Hawaii and ride big waves.

Horn was a bitchin' guy, but he worked at some terrible goddamn engineering job at Northrop—wore a suit and tie and large-rimmed glasses. A tough guy, he spent all his free time running, pumping weights and getting in shape for the day that he would find himself in the Islands, surfing big waves. He never made it, though. He never really had enough time. The couple of times he did go over there he would miss the big surf and come home totally frustrated by the whole deal. He wanted it so badly.

So, at the shop, we got to drinking wine—Horn wasn't a big drinker—and talking about Lunada Bay. It was breaking at about fifteen feet. By this time it was about three in the afternoon and we were getting pretty shit-faced. I told Kit that I had a special workout for getting in shape for big waves. What you did, I said, was tie yourself into a big truck tire innertube, paddle out at Lunada Bay, get yourself right in the impact zone, then try to catch a wave backwards. There, with your wine bottle and your innertube, you drink and wait for a wave to break on you. If you lose your bottle of wine or if you quit drinking, you're automatically disqualified.

Kit had drunk enough to believe me. And I was far enough along to be stoked on the idea. So we did it. We got two big truck tire innertubes and two fresh gallons of Red Mountain wine and went to Lunada Bay. It was near dusk as we ran down the trail. We were fired up and the whole situation turned competitive.

We paddled out in our tubes and sat right in the impact zone. A fifteen-foot set comes through and pounds the living shit out of both of us. We're laughing anyway, having a great time. Kit loses his inner tube, but holds onto his wine bottle. I'm getting a little concerned about him, but he just laughs. He had drunk about half his wine. I think the only thing keeping him afloat was the half-empty bottle.

By the time we decided to go in, the sun had gone down and I couldn't find Kit on shore. I'm walking along the beach, and it's pitch dark. I finally find him in a tide pool. He'd drug himself there and was still lying face-down, his head pointing towards the ocean. He was real screwed up; his face and body were a mass of bloody cuts. The tide was coming in and he was barfing as his head bobbed up and down in the tide pool.

Kit was a big man, weighed a couple hundred pounds. I tried to roll him out of the tidepool but couldn't. The best I could do was grab him by the ankles and drag him up the rocks, just to get his head out of the water so he wouldn't drown. I carried over a couple of big rocks, rolled one under each of his armpits and told him I was going for help.

I climbed up the path to the road and hitchhiked to a phone. I called Horn's house and somehow the message got through that Kit was lying face-down in a tide pool at Lunada Bay. His wife just went berserk. She thought he'd drowned. At this point, the cops were called in.

In the meantime, Kit comes to and starts walking up the trail. In the process of doing this, he slips and falls in some dog crap. So now he has blood and crap all over him, and he remembers that a friend of his lives at the Point at Lunada Bay. All he can think of is looking up this lifelong friend. After all, it's Christmas Eve. He stumbles into the guy's house and collapses on the couch, looking—and smelling—like shit. They call his wife, and she comes to pick him up.

For years afterwards, if the name of Greg Noll was spoken in Kit Horn's house, the woman would go into a total rage. I haven't seen the man since, and that happened in the early '60s.

Not too long ago, I was at E.T. Surfboards, a shop in Hermosa Beach owned by Eddie Talbot, a young guy who once worked for me and who became like a son to me. While I was there, a kid came up and asked me if I would tell him the story about Kit Horn at Lunada Bay. I guess it's become one of those surf stories that gets carried on from one surf generation to another.

Horn wasn't the only one to come out of that night in bad shape. I awoke on Christmas morning with the world's worst hangover. Beverly's parents were there. My two older sons, Tate and Rhyn, were waiting for me to get up so they could open their presents. When I finally dragged my carcass out of bed and came into the living room, everybody was glaring at me. "Can we open our presents now, Papa?"

For quite some time, life for many of us was nothing more than trying to out-prank the other guy. Surfing wasn't big business. It was just pursuit of fun. We didn't take each other or ourselves very seriously. I got a real kick out of competing with other guys such as José Angel, Ricky Grigg, Peter Cole, Buzzy Trent and George Downing. They all were such interesting individuals. I would try to do goofy little things to catch them off-guard when we were out in the water.

José Angel, who was probably the gutsiest of us all, was kind of a quiet guy. Didn't shout, scream or strut for the cameras. He took his surfing seriously. He loved the sport and the competition among the guys. One time, he and I were surfing at Laniakea. It was my last day in the Islands that season, and I had a plane to catch at one o'clock. I had it timed out so that I could stay in the water until the very last minute, then hurry in and change, drive to the airport and catch the flight.

This giant wave came towards us. I knew I couldn't make it. It was a terrifying deal, but I couldn't resist it. I turned to José and calmly said, "See you next year, José," took about four strokes and disappeared down the front of this ridiculous wave. Somehow or other, I got down the face and, instead of losing my board like I thought I would, I smoked out in front of the wave just as it hit a deep spot and backed up into the whitewater. I came flying out of the soup and belly-slid in the rest of the way.

The next year, as soon as I saw José, he said, "What ever happened to you on that wave?" It had worked on him all year long, just like I had hoped it would. I always liked to leave him with something to screw up his mind. He couldn't believe that I would take off so late on a wave like that, and he knew the odds were way against my hanging on to my board. He said, "I was waiting for your board to pop up and I never saw it. Then I saw you walking up the beach."

At one time, both Peter Cole and José Angel taught at the Punahou school in Honolulu. They had to drive past Waimea about six o'clock every morning on their way to work. We had a deal worked out where they would call me in California if it looked like a big day was coming up at the Bay. I kept all my stuff packed and left my big-wave board at Henry Preece's house. Since Hawaii was three hours ahead of California time, I could catch an early flight from the Mainland and be in Hawaii, in the water, by early afternoon. Alan Chang would pick me up at the airport.

I only had hit Waimea on a few occasions the very day it was coming up. Usually I'd arrive in Hawaii and take several weeks to warm up. Catch some waves, break in easy. It's quite a transition from four-to-six-foot California waves to twenty-foot-plus waves in Hawaii.

One particular morning, José calls me and says, "Jeeeez, Greg, it's coming! You'd better get over here!"

I caught the earliest flight I could get. Alan Chang picked me up, took me to Henry's to get my board and we headed for Waimea.

It had been six months since I had been in the Islands. This was the first day of the winter season. I paddled out just as a giant set rolled in. I saw Peter scratching for the first wave. He dropped down and looked like an ant as he smoked across the face of the wave. I thought, "Christ! That wave looked bigger than normal." It was.

I kept paddling out, spun around and took off on the next wave. It was even bigger. I remember thinking to myself, "Goddammit, I'm not going to let Peter get away with this." It was straight up and down and I was late getting into the wave. The ass end of the board dropped out from under me and I free-fell from top to bottom. I ate it somethin' fierce.

I think it meant more to me to psych out Peter than it did to make the wave. Peter was a hell of a waterman, but he had some shred of sanity. José would practically kill himself before he'd let anybody get the best of him. And Ricky was usually too smart to get sucked into these head games. Each one of these guys was interesting and complex in his own way, and I just loved to mess with their brains.

105

PETER COLE
Surfer, Teacher, Mathematician

Greg has to have the most guts of anyone I've ever known. He'd fly in from California and head right for Waimea that same day. The biggest wave I've ever seen anyone take off on was at Waimea, and Greg was the one going for it. He had just flown in from California and had started hyperventilating like he always did in big surf. There was a huge wave coming and you could see there was no way he could get down more than a third of it, but he went for it anyway. I swear, he took off with his eyes shut. I asked Greg about it afterward and he said, "You don't think I'd take off on a wave like that with my eyes open, do you?" I've been telling that story for years.

I have more fun now than I ever had, surfing Sunset Beach with my son, Peter junior. I've really gotten conservative in my older years. I guess the kids out there today feel sorry for me—they give me waves. Greg never gave me a wave in his life!

Greg, José Angel and I had a friendly competition going. Greg and José were always jockeying for the inside position. You'd see them at Waimea, coming from way the other side of the point, streaking all the way across a wave. On some days, Greg would sit right in the middle of the rest of us. But on other days, his sixth sense told him there was a bigger wave out there. He'd paddle way outside and wait for it. I'd hear him start to hyperventilate. That was my cue that a big one was coming, so I'd paddle out and join him. Greg was my lineup.

I started surfing in Santa Cruz in the fifties. Kit Horn, Buzzy Trent and I were in grammar school together and they got me started surfing. I watched Buzzy for years. He beat me up about twenty times. I had an identical twin brother, Corny—Buzzy beat up both of us. What got me to the Islands was seeing surf movies of Greg, Buffalo and Henry riding Haleiwa and Sunset Beach. I'll never forget seeing Henry coming down the face of a perfect twelve-foot wave at Haleiwa, then he turns around backwards on the board and throws the wave a kiss. I thought, "That's it. That's where I'm going." I've been here ever since.

RICKY GRIGG

There is an old Greg Noll Surfboards ad that shows me, Fred Hemmings, Felipe Pomar and Greg with our Greg Noll surfboards out in front of my house on the North Shore. I rode mine when I won the 1967 Duke Kahanamoku. I never let Greg forget that I rode one of his boards to beat him in a contest.

The interesting part of the friendly competition between Greg and me is that people always used to say to me, "You know, Ricky, it's those trunks you wear that make you so well known. Not only did you do all this surfing, you also built boards and you were part of the history of surfing." I think I have been confused with Greg Noll more times than I have been recognized for myself. I would just shrug my shoulders and chuckle inside, because they thought I was Greg Noll. The reason for the confusion is that "Greg" is the name that seems to have stuck with most people, and that's how my last name is pronounced.

The atmosphere among all of us was highly competitive, and yet there was a difference between and among us that you don't find today. That is, I can never remember once being angry or mad at Greg, Peter, Buzzy, Georgie, José or any of our contemporaries. We were happy to see the other guy win, to see him catch the wave of the day. We wanted to be better, or at least as good as the next guy, and this competitive spirit helped us be as good as we were.

Today, the competition is a lot more ruthless, more cutthroat. Guys fight and there is a lot of hostility out on the water. We didn't feel that way about one another. There were, of course, confrontations. It would have been hard to surf with someone for twenty years and not run over them or have them run over you in the water, at least once or twice.

DICK METZ
Surfer, Founder of Hobie Sports Stores

Greg was such a prankster. He loved to incite insurrections and then stand back in the corner and giggle while he watched the outcome.

One of Greg's little games is to thump you on the head with his finger cocked like you would to shoot a marble. It hurts, especially if you aren't expecting it. One time, he and Pat Curren met for breakfast at the Stuffed T-Shirt in Newport Beach, a little back-street diner we all liked. They were sitting at the counter, eating breakfast. Pat's a man of very few words. Rarely looks you in the eye when he talks to you. So he's sitting there, quietly eating his breakfast, with Greg on one side of him and a big gnarly-looking fisherman sitting on the other side. Greg reaches around behind Pat and thumps this fisherman on the head. The fisherman jumps, looks around, can't see anyone else near enough to have done it, so he lights into Pat.

Pat hits the floor with the fisherman on top of him, ready to pound him into the ground. Greg is getting a big kick out of this, but finally decides to help out his buddy and pulls the fisherman off Pat. Exit fisherman. Greg helps Pat to his feet. Pat watches the fisherman leave, then turns back to the counter, shaking himself off and mumbling, "Gee, I wonder what got into that guy."

Greg felt so guilty that he let years go by before he ever told Pat that he was the one who thumped the fisherman.

———————————

THE THUMB

Ricky James was an excellent shaper who worked for me for several years before he started his own board shop. One day, in our old shop on Pacific Coast Highway, Ricky was sawing center strips for boards and talking to one of his buddies at the same time. I was about fifteen feet away and I told him, "Ricky, goddammit, pay attention to what you're doing." He says, "I am, I am." He's telling stories to this guy and the saw is whining yeoooow, yeoooow, yeoooow as it cuts off center strips.

Suddenly I hear the saw stop and Ricky yells, "Oh, God!" I rush over, and there's his thumb on the floor. He had sawed it off almost at the base. I grab a paper towel, scoop up the thumb and take Ricky to the hospital. All the time we're driving, I'm talking to him, trying to keep him from going into shock.

"Do you think they can sew it back on?" he asks me.

"Oh yeah, they got modern-day medicine, no sweat, Rick. Just settle down, everything is going to be just fine. They'll sew it back on. You may have a little scar but everything is going to be O.K."

I'm driving and he's sitting on the passenger side and the thumb is between us, on the seat. While we're talking, Ricky keeps looking down at it as though the thumb is a third person in the car.

As soon as we get to the hospital, they take Ricky into Emergency. I've got the thumb and Ricky is clasping the stub and the doctor walks in. Ricky says, "I'm so glad you're here. Are you going to be able to sew my thumb back on, Doc?"

The doctor had the worst bedside manner of any doctor I've ever met. He says, "No, it wouldn't do any good. We could sew it back on, but it would just turn black and fall off in a few days. There's no use in even trying."

Now Ricky is really going into shock over the whole situation and he says, "Doc, please. I don't know what my girlfriend will think of me. I don't care if it works or anything. Just sew it back on so it looks good. I don't care if it works."

The doctor talked to him for a while. Of course, they didn't sew the thumb back on. I saw that a nurse had the thumb and was going to dispose of it. I said, "Do you mind if I take that with me?" She thought it was kind of an odd request, but she gave it to me. I didn't tell Ricky.

After they got Ricky bandaged up I took him home, gave him a couple of beers and left him there to relax. Then I went back to the shop and mixed up a nice, slow batch of resin in a Dixie cup. Dropped the thumb in it. Let it set up, then took off the Dixie cup. It was absolutely perfect. Looked like a paperweight with a thumb suspended in it.

Ricky was off work for a while, so we used the thumb as a sort of novelty item. In the inner shop, we stuck it in the showcase where we had fins, wax, skateboard accessories and . . . a thumb. People browsing in the shop would look in the showcase and say, "Hey, take a look at this fake thumb." Then they'd take a closer look and say, "Jesus Christ, this isn't a fake. Look, you can see dirt under the fingernail."

The thumb got to be such a conversation piece that guys started coming in from all over the place just to see it. I came into the shop one Saturday and there must have been eight or ten guys shoulder-deep at the showcase, trying to get a glimpse of the thumb.

Meanwhile, Ricky gets wind that his thumb is on display. I hear he's mad, so I put away the thumb for safekeeping. He comes in asking for his thumb. We had a giant argument about whose thumb it was. I said, "I found it." Ricky said, "I don't care. You're not supposed to put a guy's thumb on display."

We used to freak out people, especially girls, with the thumb. We'd say to a girl, "Hold out your hand. I want to show you something." And we'd put the thumb in the Dixie cup in her hand, remove the Dixie cup and watch a hundred expressions go across her face. She wouldn't know whether to drop it or throw it or what.

Ricky and I argued about The Thumb for nearly two years. I still have it. It's buried in a box somewhere.

INDUSTRY AND IMAGE

A lot of guys who used to work with me went into business on their own. Eddie Talbot, who now owns E.T. Surfboards in Hermosa Beach, came to work at the shop as a salesman in the late sixties when he was just a kid. Pat Ryan, who everyone still calls Gumby, started shaping for me around the same time and now shapes for Eddie. Gumby is also a terrific sailboarder.

Of course, Ricky James, of the thumb fame, went on to make boards under his own name. And Wayne Land, one of the original Windansea surfers, now owns a bar in the Islands. Harold Iggy now works with Ricky Naish at Naish Hawaii, designing sailboards for Mistral. Ben Aipa, a great big-wave surfer in his own right, is still surfing and promoting contests.

A young Hawaiian surfer named Craig Sugihara came over from the Islands a few times to check out how the business was run. Craig was one of the young kids who used to hang around at Buff's house. In the mid-sixties, he worked as a laminator for Charlie Galanto at Greg Noll Surfboards in Honolulu. He and another one of my shapers and good friend, Tak Kawahara, teamed up to start Town & Country Surf Designs, now one of the more successful surf companies in the industry. Because of my relationship with Buff, I just opened up the shop to Craig to help him and Tak get started.

We made boards for lots of the guys in the Islands. When Charlie Galanto opened Greg Noll Surfboards in Honolulu in 1965, we had a total lip lock on the big-wave-board business for many years. It was the perfect combination—my recognition from surfing big waves on the North Shore combined with Charlie's ability to wheel and deal, not to mention his surfing expertise.

111

Before George Downing opened his own shop, he spent a lot of time at Charlie's shop. George actually endorsed our slot-bottom board at one time. One of our ads in *Surfer* in 1966 shows a picture of George and a testimonial. I was very honored.

By the mid-sixties, the surf industry was booming. We built a twenty-thousand-square-foot factory on a lot a couple blocks off Pacific Coast Highway in Hermosa Beach. We kept the retail store up on the highway. The factory was for offices and board production only. The building was a city block long. It started with the foam room, where foam for the surfboard blanks was formulated and then blown into one of several different molds. After that, the foam blanks were split in two so that a center strip of wood could be glued into the boards for reinforcement. From there, the blanks were moved into the shaping room on carts. There were eight shaping stalls. We were set up to produce up to forty boards a day, or two hundred a week.

After the boards were shaped, they continued on the carts into the laminating room, where there was a sea of tables. The room was temperature-controlled with separate work tables for each laminator. In one corner was the sanding area with a huge blower that could remove twenty-one thousand cubic feet of dusty air per minute. The next room also had a bunch of work tables for glassing. It was heat-controlled, with a complete air change every one and a half minutes. In the last room, the boards were polished and then crated for shipping.

It was quite an operation. At times we exceeded two hundred boards a week. During surfing's heyday in the sixties, we had sixty-three East Coast dealers that we had to keep supplied, in addition to other dealers on the Mainland and in Hawaii. I'd go back there two or three times a year to attend store openings and pep rallies at local schools, and to judge surf contests. I hated it more than anything in the world. The people were nice, but I dreaded dealing with all that promotional crap.

Other Recollections

LAURA

I had worked as a secretary at the retail shop on the Coast Highway for a few years before the factory opened. Then all the offices were moved to the factory. Part of my job was to keep track of the Red Book. This book contained the secret formula that Greg and his father, Ash, had worked up for producing the foam blanks used in the surfboard operation. Greg was one of the few manufacturers who made his own blanks. By then, most of them were buying blanks from Clark Foam.

Whenever they needed to change the formula to make a board heavier, lighter, stronger or whatever, I'd call Ash and tell him what we wanted. He'd work it out and give me the instructions on how to alter the formula. I recorded it in the book and kept it under lock and key in a file.

Other Recollections

TAK KAWAHARA
Cofounder and President of T&C Surf Designs

I grew up surfing in Malibu during the late fifties. I started out patching surfboards, then worked my way up through laminating to shaping. Over the years, I worked for several different surfboard manufacturers, including Con Colburn, Dewey Weber, Hap Jacobs and Greg Noll. I was fortunate to have been surrounded by many great shapers of that time and learned a lot from them. I shaped boards up until the early seventies.

Back then, the typical surfboard factory was tiny and always dirty. Full of foam dust and resin, which would build up on your clothes and shoes. Greg's big factory was a state-of-the-art operation from start to finish. I remember thinking, when we first moved in, "Everything is so new and clean!" Greg's office was plush, nicely carpeted with several tropical fish tanks. The first time I went into his office I was covered with foam dust and resin. I thought the least I could do was take off my shoes. This became a sort of tradition, to take off your shoes, Hawaiian-style, no matter who you were, before going into Greg's office.

The Hawaiian style is a big part of Greg. For all practical purposes, Greg is Hawaiian. I think everybody adopts the Hawaiian style when they go to Hawaii, but Greg especially. He picks up their way of talkin', he loves Hawaiian food and he loves talkin' stories Hawaiian-style with all da boys.

Guys who worked at surfboard factories did it for one reason—as a means to surf. You were close to something that you really loved. In the early days, the best part about it was, when the surf was up, nobody was working. By the time Greg opened up his new factory, the surf work ethic had changed. No matter if the surf was up, you had to work. Heavy demand from the East Coast meant that you had to meet your shipment deadlines. Making surfboards had become big business.

To combat the urge among us workers to grab our boards and hit the surf, there was a huge picture in the laminating room of Greg dressed in a sombrero and serape, holding a big machete. Underneath the picture, in large letters, it said, "WATCHETH, FOR YE KNOW NOT WHEN THE MASTER COMETH." With Big Brother always lurking not too far away, we worked!

During early production of the Mickey Dora Cat board, Wayne Land was the exclusive shaper. As demand increased for Cat boards, other shapers got involved, including myself. The step deck on the Cat board was copied by several other surfboard makers. Rich Harbour called his model the Spoon.

There was, and still is, a camaraderie among the guys who were around in the old days. We all surfed and worked together. Today there are so many people involved in the surf industry that you know very few. Back in those days, guys were rowdy without the drug element we see today. There was more fun to it. In partying and image presence, there were some real legends back in those days. Greg ranks right up there with the best of them. His size alone was something to talk about. He was larger than life and made such great contributions to the sport. He was one of the great pioneers, not only in surfboard building but in big-wave riding as well.

———————————

I hated seeing the drug scene shift into high gear like it did. I feel a little self-righteous standing on my soapbox with a bottle of beer in my hand, and I can't claim to have been a total virgin when it came to experimenting with drugs. But I can look back over the years and say that I saw a lot of neat, bright, healthy young kids who I know would have become great athletes if they hadn't gotten overly involved in drugs and gone straight down the shit chute.

With some guys, drugs became a way of life. They went through tremendous personality changes, or they died. Drugs didn't do them any good. In the same way, at certain times in my life, alcohol didn't do me any good. A lot of kids today seem to be taking themselves, their health and their education more seriously, and that's good.

In the sixties, the image of surfing started getting a little strange. People were talking about putting a ban on surfing between San Francisco and San Diego. They also talked about putting a five-dollar licensing fee on surfboards, but that didn't go over, either.

The bad press really contributed to the wild, lifestyle image that surfing had picked up. Surfers would read all this stuff and say, "That sounds really neat. I'm going to get me a hearse and go do that. Get me some beer and thirteen-year-old girls and jam them in the back seat."

The swastika became a symbol of some surfers just because it pissed off people. It was a rebellious act. That's why Mickey Dora painted swastikas all over his boards. Most surfers didn't even know what it meant. It was just another way of shaking the pillars of society, something we excelled in doing.

Over the years I heard a lot of guys say, "I'm going to get in shape for the Islands." They'd start running on the beach, swimming, working out. Eddie Talbot, one of my younger salesmen, was so stoked on the idea of riding big waves that I finally invited him to go to the Islands in '69. He had himself so psyched up that I wasn't sure what was going to happen.

We hit Sunset Beach on an average day of crisp, twelve-to-fourteen-foot waves. When you first paddle out through the rip at Sunset Beach, you can't see the outside break for several minutes. You hear the waves popping and growling before you get a good look at them. Eddie's eyes got bigger and bigger as we got closer and closer to the break. Once we got out there, he finally picked a wave and took off. The wave snapped and he went flying on his backside halfway down the front of the wave just as the lip came over and drove him underwater. Eddie finally surfaced and said, "Christ Almighty, this isn't at all what I thought it was going to be."

It really was my fault. I should have broken him in a little slower. But maybe it was just as well. Once Eddie got stoked on something, there was no stopping him. Instead of devoting himself to surfing in the Islands, he went back to the Mainland and opened one of the most successful surf shops in California.

EDDIE TALBOT
Surfer, Owner of E. T. Surfboards

In the mid-sixties, when I was seventeen, I was surfing and living out of my car, hustling boards in the water. I had a deal with Bing Copeland. For every guy I'd send in to his shop to buy a board, he'd pay me five bucks.

Eventually, I started sending guys to Greg's shop too. I sent so many customers his way that Greg asked to meet me. I was all fired up, full of ideas. I told Greg he should start a surf team. He said, "Do it." So I did.

I ended up working in the retail store and had a falling out with one of Greg's salesmen. So I moved to the factory and sold boards and materials from there. I ended up selling more there than I did in retail.

The first and last time I went to Hawaii to ride the North Shore was with Greg in '69. We went to Sunset Beach and Greg asked me how big I thought the waves were. I said, "Aw, about six feet." Greg said, with a sly look, "I'll meet you out there."

You don't know until you get out there how bad it can be. The waves were over ten feet but seemed much bigger, and I got pounded.

I didn't work for Greg during the shop's heyday. I was there as he was winding down his business. Toward the end, Laura and I practically ran the shop. I learned a lot and was able to open my own shop after Greg's closed down. I started E. T. Surfboards in '72, with two thousand dollars.

Greg was the closest thing to a father I've ever had. I was never real close to my real father, and when you're seventeen or so, you need a role model. Greg was a model to me, both of what to do and what not to do. Now, I've had a chance to repay him by bringing his son, Rhyn, into my shop and having Gumby help teach him to shape boards. Rhyn is carrying on the tradition by opening his own surf shop in Crescent City.

DICK METZ

In the early sixties there weren't that many retail surf stores anywhere. Most of the guys making boards sold them where they made them, so the common surf shop was also a surfboard factory. Hobie Alter's first store in Dana Point was like that, until he moved the board-making operation down the road a ways and converted the store to retail only.

In 1961 I opened the first retail surf shop in the Islands, Hobie Sports, in Honolulu. There was another surf shop there at the time, Joe "Kitchens" Kuala's Inter Island Surfboards, but this was also a factory. At the Hobie Sports shop, you could order a custom board, but most of the inventory was ready to go.

Over the next couple of years, as different surfboard manufacturers from the Mainland came to the Islands, they saw how well Hobie Sports was doing and decided that they wanted to do the same. Some of them asked me to carry their boards in my shop, but since it was called Hobie Sports and specialized in Hobie Surfboards, I thought it might be a conflict of interest.

To solve that problem and also be able to do business with other surfboard manufacturers, I opened a second store called Surf Line Hawaii and acted as a distributor for various Mainland board makers, including Reynolds Yater, Dewey Weber, Don Hansen, Bing Copeland, Gordon & Smith and Greg Noll. This gave kids in Hawaii access to all the major California surfboard manufacturers. I took in a partner, Dave Rochlen. Soon afterwards, he and his wife started the Jams surftrunk craze and devoted all their energy to the clothing end of the business. So we brought over Freddie Schwartz, a friend of Dave's from Santa Monica, to run the shop.

Greg was more into Hawaii and big-wave riding than the other manufacturers. His boards were getting lost among the supermarket of surfboards that we had created at Surf Line Hawaii. In the mid-sixties, Greg decided to let Charlie Galanto represent him like I represented Hobie. Charlie opened Greg Noll Surfboards in Honolulu. Greg and

Charlie made a good team. Charlie was very loud and vocal. He'd get on the radio and promote the shop, really talking up the big-wave deal.

Each of us carved out our own niche in the business. Hobie Sports dominated the general surf market for a while, but Greg really owned the big-wave market.

Greg threw the greatest party of all time when he opened his surfboard factory in Hermosa Beach. He invited just about everybody in the surf industry to an open-house party at the factory. Although all of us were rivals in the business, we were also good friends. At that time, I think everyone had as much of a market share as he could handle.

While the South Bay area had its own collection of super surf stars, farther south, the Dana Point/Capistrano Beach area wasn't hurting for its own luminaries. Hobie had many great surfers on his surf team, from Phil Edwards and Joey Cabell to a young upstart named Corky Carroll. Other well-known surfers in the area included surf movie producer Bruce Brown; surf fabric suppliers Walter and Flippy Hoffman; *Surfer* publisher John Severson; and foam-blank supplier Grubby Clark. We were known in the industry as the Dana Point Mafia.

We thought, since everyone called us that, why not go to the party as the Dana Point Mafia? We all grew mustaches and raided local thrift shops for old clothes. The guys wore twenties-style double-breasted suits, old hats and carried toy guns, while the wives and girlfriends dressed up in flapper outfits. We each chose what gangster character we wanted to be—except for Phil Edwards. He decided that he would be good-guy Elliot Ness. We hired a bus to drive us to Hermosa Beach.

We all met at the Hobie store in Dana Point early in the afternoon and started drinking while we waited for the bus. By the time we crawled onto the bus we were loaded. We made several stops at local bars on the way to Hermosa Beach, and walked into Greg's party thoroughly drunk. He had really outdone himself, laid out a great buffet dinner and open bar. He had a whole program planned for the evening, including a bogus awards presentation—things like elevator shoes for Dewey Weber and a time bomb for Hobie so that Greg could get all of Hobie's business when it went off.

About all I clearly remember is dumping a whole bowl of macaroni salad on Mike Stange, which started a food fight around and under the table. It was one of the all-time great get-togethers.

BEVERLY

What made Greg and I such a great team for so many years was the fact that I'm conservative and Greg is no-holds-barred. He'd crash head-long into things and I'd go along behind him, picking up the pieces.

Laura and I have been friends forever, it seems. There have been so many times when Laura has been my best friend in the world. Our friendship developed when she came to work at the shop. Her relationship with Greg just happened. You don't have control over who you fall in love with. Everyone likes to think that they do, but you don't.

When I confronted Greg and Laura, it was upsetting at first for all of us, but eventually the issue was just shelved. There was no hard-and-fast agreement. We just decided, "O.K., let's see what happens." At that point in time, Greg was an enormously strong energy field. It could be exhausting to be around him. It got to the point where, when I knew he would be at Laura's, I looked forward to having an evening or two to myself.

Laura had been working at the shop for a little over a year when we first got involved. A bunch of us were at a party one night and I asked her to dance. The twist was the big dance then. I'd had a few beers, every-body was dancing and about halfway through the dance I just stopped, grabbed Laura and started kissing her. It was the damnedest thing, I just couldn't help myself.

About two weeks later, things just started happening between us. We really never did get caught, unless you consider being busted after seven years as getting caught. Beverly walked into Laura's house and caught me in my skivvies, cleaning the fish tank. I had built this huge tank out of a jet canopy and the only way you could clean it was to get inside. That's what I was doing when Beverly walked in. What a way to get caught. Standing inside a six-foot-high fish tank, looking like a goddamn grouper blowing bubbles and trying to explain myself. Later Beverly

119

asked me what I wanted to do about the situation. I said I would try to do whatever I could to keep everyone happy.

By the time we moved to Crescent City, Beverly and Laura had become good friends, and still are. I consider myself to be very fortunate to have two such very special people care enough to spend part of their lives with me. There were many times over the years when people just couldn't understand our unusual lifestyle. I always figured that was their problem, not ours. I think people are threatened when you don't fit into one of their little cubbyholes.

STREET-FIGHTING MEN

Other Recollections

BRUCE BROWN

In the Islands you have to pay your dues before you're accepted by the Hawaiians. You have to be nice. When we first started going over there, the natives weren't too crazy about us haoles. This is still somewhat true today. If it hadn't been for our friendship with Buff and Henry, we'd all have been killed forty times over.

Of course, when Greg got a couple of drinks in him, he wasn't much different than some moke at a party who's had too much to drink and suddenly decides to go after the "focking haole." As things got drunker at whatever bar we were all congregated in, we'd see that it was time to leave and we'd try to get Greg to go with us. He wouldn't. He'd stay, the only haole in the bar. And he'd usually end up in a fight.

One time, Greg and Mickey Muñoz took a couple gallons of wine down to the beach near Haleiwa in the late afternoon, planning to sit on the seawall and enjoy the rest of the day. Eventually, a carload of mokes pulled up and started talking to them. Greg and Muñoz make the mistake of offering them some wine. As the mokes started feeling the wine, things got a little hostile and Greg told Muñoz that he was going for help. Here's Greg, this big hulk of a guy, leaving Muñoz, a guy about half his size, to deal with the mokes while Greg goes back for reinforcements.

Greg came back to the house we were sharing with a few friends and asked me and a couple of buddies to come help him out. We found

121

Muñoz, who at that time was fond of wearing just a sheet with a hole in it, leaning against a tree. The mokes had punched him out and then just left him propped up there, against this tree. Greg went over and touched his arm and Muñoz just fell over, flat on his face. Greg nearly died laughing. He thought that was the funniest thing he'd ever seen.

Other Recollections

SONNY VARDEMAN

The Hawaiian style is, you have to be pretty rough-tough or you get run over. Greg caught on to this when he went to high school in Hawaii, and fell in with it. He was always trim and had massive shoulders from paddling, but throughout high school, he wasn't physically aggressive at all. He was outgoing and sociable, went to parties. But, if a ruckus started, Greg wouldn't have anything to do with it. He'd get the hell out of there. All the rough-tough stuff came later, as he spent more time in Hawaii and got into big-wave surfing. As he matured and became a successful surfboard manufacturer, Greg's aggressiveness toned down somewhat, although he was always up for a party.

I was with Mike Stange one night when he got ripped. We were sitting in a very nice bar, one of those with a real bitchin' mirror on the wall behind the glasses. Mike had had just a little too much to drink and started muttering about some problems he was having at home. Then he just picked up his beer bottle and threw it. The mirror cracked into a giant spider web. The bartender sunk down behind the counter, expecting the worse was yet to come, but Mike jumped off his seat and ran out. I took off after him but he was too fast for me. He ran madly down the street, stopped at a metal newsstand, picked it up and threw it against a plate-glass window. Another spider web.

He took off towards his house, but, as drunk as he was, he ran up the steps to the wrong one. I was still several steps behind him. Some stranger came to the door and Mike made mincemeat out of him. The cops came to Mike's aid about that time. There was nothing I could do.

I visited Mike in County Jail. He was wearing these little slippers, sweatpants and a straitjacket. The look on Mike's face said, "Get me out of this thing and I will never drink again." For about five years, he didn't have a thing to drink. After that, if he drank at all, it was only beer. It was a turning point in his life.

Nowadays guys go to the Islands and break two, three boards or more, riding the winter surf. Modern boards are lighter and slimmer. In my day if you broke a board in half it was a big deal. Like it was a black mark against your skill as a surfboard designer.

I was the first to use lightweight sticks for center strips in surfboards, to get the weight down. The old eleven-foot guns weighed forty-five to fifty pounds. They were double glassed and had the heavier, three-quarter-inch redwood sticks in them for reinforcement.

In the sixties I blew my own foam. My dad figured out the formula and continually revised it, trying to come up with a lighter-density foam. I also single-glassed the boards, used aircraft-grade spruce for the center sticks, messed with the board design—anything to get the weight down and still have some performance. As a result my boards were riding better, but every once in a while one would break.

At that time a lot of the big-wave surfers on the North Shore were riding my boards. Dick Brewer, who went on to become a well-known shaper in his own right, was up-and-coming then and trying to find his niche. He opened a little shop in Haleiwa and put one of the boards I had made for José Angel in his window. Trouble was, the board had broken in half one day when José had it out in some big surf. Brewer had somehow got his hands on the two halves and put them in his window with my logo sticker showing. It was a real back-biting, chicken-shit thing to do and I was really pissed.

It so happened that I was able to confront Brewer one night, when Mike Stange and I went to a party at Warren "Tubby" Harlow's house, right on the point at Waimea. We both got a little smashed. Brewer was there, so I asked him what the hell he thought he was doing, putting my broken board in his shop window. He ignored me and called Mike an undesirable name, so I asked Brewer to go outside with me and settle this dispute. He wouldn't go, so I popped him right where he stood. His wife started screeching like a banshee and then talked some other guy into trying to hammer me over the head with a beer bottle. The whole thing turned into diarrhea and the cops were called.

123

Mike and I decided then and there that this would be a good time to take a tour of the other islands. We left before the cops arrived and headed for Maui, where we spent three very forgettable days. Then, on to Lanai for a day. Lanai is not much more than a pineapple field with a little hill at one end. There's one town where most of the population lives. We talked to these elderly Japanese people who had lived on Lanai all their lives and had never been off the island. We couldn't believe it. Talk about island fever. We could hardly wait to get off Lanai and back to Oahu.

Our rental car ran out of gas on the way back to the airport. We siphoned what we thought was gas out of a tractor, and realized too late that it was diesel. We abandoned the car and hitched a ride back to the airport.

Before going back to Oahu we stopped over in Molokai and discovered that the locals had never before seen a real surfboard. At one bar we visited, all the guys crowded around to touch and examine our boards. And here we were, only thirty miles across the channel from the greatest surf spots in the world!

When we got to the Molokai airport all we had in our pockets were our airline tickets back to Oahu and enough change for a couple of hot dogs. We were so starved that we heaped on all the mustard and relish those hot dogs could hold. I ate the rest of the relish straight from the jar.

By the time we finally rolled back into Haleiwa, I had decided to go apologize to Brewer. As soon as I showed up, his wife called the cops and they came and hauled me off to the jug. Even the Hawaiian cops couldn't understand why some haole would press charges against somebody who had just taken one shot. That's all I did, just backhanded Brewer. It happened to break his nose and he sued me for a hundred and fifty thousand dollars. What an asshole. Eventually he dropped the lawsuit and we got along O.K. Life's too short for all that crap.

ADVENTURES WITH DICK AND GREG

Other Recollections

RICHARD GRAHAM
Founder of INTERNATIONAL SURFING *Magazine*

I met Greg in the early sixties when I was selling advertising for and editing Petersen Publishing's *Petersen's Surfing* magazine. I sold an ad to Greg and also ended up including him in several editorials. After that we became friends, hung out together in the Islands and here on the Mainland.

I've bodysurfed and surfed most of my life. I started surfing in Malibu in '53, then drifted to Dana Point and Doheny, bought my first surfboard from Hobie's shop in Dana Point. I had written and published a softcover book called *Surfing Made Easy,* which was technically edited by Hobie Alter. It sold briefly on newsstands and for about two years through various surf shops nationally, including Hobie's.

I also worked for a time in Petersen's data-processing department. There I got the idea to start up my own surf magazine. I rounded up a few partners: Tooley Clark and another old-time South Bay surfer provided the financial backing, while Leroy Grannis did the photography. I was the only full-time employee, the "chief cook and editor." We launched *International Surfing* in 1964. The "International" portion of the name was dropped by new owners around 1971. In 1989, *Surfing* magazine celebrated its twenty-fifth anniversary.

Through *International Surfing,* I started the Hall of Fame of Surfing. Greg Noll, Buzzy Trent and George Downing were among the first inductees, along with Duke Kahanamoku, Mike Doyle, Mickey Dora, Phil Edwards, Dewey Weber, Pete Peterson and Hoppy Swartz. All these men were surfing pioneers in their own right.

Greg was serious about his work. As a businessman, Greg planned his time well. He got his work done and still had time to surf and play. He made a lot of big-wave boards for the Islands and did a good business there. He was fairly articulate and possessed a wealth of knowledge about Hawaii—especially about the waves and the boards needed to ride them. He's one of the most thorough people I have ever met.

Greg and I were invited to Peru in 1966 as judges for the annual International Surfing Championships, which took place at Club Kon-Tiki in Lima and at a major surf spot called Punta Rocas, "Point of Rocks." I think, on that trip, Greg and I really cemented our friendship.

It was a wild adventure all the way. We started out on a flight we later named the Flight of the Varig. It took us twenty-six hours to fly from Los Angeles to Lima, Peru. The plane kept breaking down and having to land. During one unscheduled, eight-hour stop in Mexico City, they ran out of food on the plane and fed us candy instead. Finally, the decision was made to lay over in Mexico City to do repairs and to feed the passengers. We were bused into town to a hotel, but as soon as we arrived, the local *federales* made us turn around and head back to the airport. We didn't know what was going on. While the bus was stopped at a traffic signal, Greg jumped out and ran to a roadside fruit stand. He bought all the fruit he could carry. The bus driver couldn't believe it—horns honking, hungry passengers yelling for food . . . but Greg was happy. I also remember being locked up in the plane with a group of Japanese tourists who were suffering from the Asian flu and vomiting all over the place. It was awful.

But nothing compared to the flight out of Mexico City. The plane hit a downdraft on takeoff and started doing wing wheelies. It was over on its right wing, going in circles, straight down. Greg was slammed up against the window with me half on top of him. He's yelling, "We're gonna die! We're gonna die, goddammit, this is it!"

Somehow, the plane made it to Lima. Greg and I had brought four boards each with us. I had planned to do a fashion shoot for the magazine and also had a ton of clothes with me for that. We sold everything before we came home and paid for the trip.

126

The contest lasted about a week. Felipe Pomar won on one of Greg's boards and CBS filmed it. Greg and I had fallen in with our Peruvian hosts, who were anxious to show us their best women and favorite nightclubs. We didn't see a sober evening.

Greg is called Da Bull for his tenacity and aggressiveness in big waves. I'm convinced that he also had a feeling of invulnerability in the face of death. He liked the fighting. In barroom brawls, he usually took on more than one guy, and usually whipped them. He thinks he's immortal. He proved this to me in Peru.

After a late night with our hosts at some bar, we were driving back to our hotel, hollering and joking all the way, feeling no pain. Greg leaned out the window to spit just as we passed this guy who was standing on a street corner. Bull's-eye!

The guy is really pissed off, pulls a gun and points it at Greg. The rest of us immediately hit the floor, yelling to the driver to put the pedal to the metal and get the hell out of there. But what does Greg do? He hangs out the window, waves his arms, and yells at the guy, "Go ahead and shoot, you coward!" The guy had more sense than Greg, so we survived that adventure.

When Graham and I were in Peru to judge the world championships, we took a side trip to the Andes. We had been to the Bario the night before, with a beautiful, six-foot-five-inch, dark-skinned woman—in itself, another memorable adventure.

Anyway, the next morning, we're both flying over the Andes in this chicken-shit DC-4. The oxygen masks drop down when the plane starts over the crest of the Andes, at about eighteen thousand feet. We've both got the masks to our faces. The tube to Graham's mask is lying across my lap. His hangover is worse than mine and he's also suffering from the effects of the local cuisine, so I decide to add to his discomfort by pinching off his oxygen, little by little. When he'd start to turn a bit green, I'd let up and give him a little more oxygen. He had no idea what I was doing.

Suddenly, he jumps up and runs to the head. The lovely Latin American stewardess on the flight helps him get the door open. Graham is suffering from both ends. First he sits on the toilet. Then he finds he can't get down on his knees to puke without leaving the door open. So there he is, his pants to his knees, his bare ass to the wind and his head in the toilet. All this time, the lovely Latin American stewardess is patting him on the back. God, I'd have given anything for a camera.

RICHARD GRAHAM

Greg and I always made it a point to get together on a regular basis for a good number of years. Sometimes Mike Stange would join us. I remember how we'd revert to being teenagers, buy a few six-packs of beer and take Greg's dog, Sam, along for a cat hunt.

Greg had a collection of electronic garage-door openers. We'd take these along and cruise the alleys in Hermosa Beach, punching all these different garage-door openers until somebody's garage door would fling open and, invariably, a cat would run out. We'd let Sam out of the car and then follow him down the alley, hootin' and hollerin' while Sam chased cats. Great fun.

One time in Hawaii, we were at Buff's and the surf was flat. Buff handed rifles and beer all around and we sat in the shade across from his house, shooting huge rats out of the trees. We made bets on each shot.

Greg was a wild guy, always looking for adventure and a good time. I joined him willingly. There was, and never is, a dull moment in our friendship. Greg has always been kind and gentle with his family and friends. However, he's also the eternal fraternity boy, playing gags and pranks on everyone, even to this day. Whenever we're together, I continually remind myself never to let him out of my sight.

DORA

No one surfer from the fifties and sixties has managed to create the kind of mystique that surrounded, and continues to surround, Mickey Dora. Dora worked hard to create a legendary persona for himself. This persona enabled the real Dora to hide from the rest of the world.

Different people who knew Dora have described him as sensitive, crazy and erratic. He was a colorful, unpredictable guy who loved a good caper. And he was more. Despite what anyone thought of him as a person, as a surfer, Dora was a genius. He was a tremendous athlete who surfed with a beautiful, smooth, natural style. Dora's influence can been seen in every surfer from that era who ever dared to invade Dora's home turf of Malibu. Every surfer, and even kids who didn't surf, tried to copy the way Dora walked, talked and surfed. To this day, Dora is a Malibu legend. The famous wall at the beach there always has Dora's name on it, or some saying about Dora, such as "DORA LIVES." The county comes along now and then and paints over all the graffiti on the wall, and the next day somebody has spray-painted Dora's name there again.

In fact, a couple of years ago, Laura and I and our two children, Ashlyne and Jed, were on our way back from a trip and we drove by Malibu. The kids had never been there and wanted to stop. It was a winter day, nobody on the beach. I pulled over to let the kids walk along the beach. We went to take a look at the wall, and noticed Dora's name among the graffiti. In one place, it also said, "DA BULL," and in another it said, "DA CAT IS KING." Over twenty years have gone by since Dora and I made that board together, and somebody still remembered.

Dora was a rebel. The freedom of the surfing lifestyle suited him perfectly. Although he agreed to let me make a signature board for him in the mid-sixties, he hated the surf industry, which he felt had ruined the purity of the sport. Even though I made my living making surfboards, I had to agree with him on that point.

Dora was a bright guy and had a very quick mind, but it was all turned toward the con. I talk about the capers we all loved to pull on each other—they were pretty harmless diversions. Dora's thing got so bad, so far out in the wrong direction, that the capers became reality and his whole life turned to conning people to get by. It was rumored that he got caught writing bad checks, using stolen or forged credit cards. Some people said that he'd get into Hollywood parties by passing as an actor and then things like fur coats and valuables that had been left in the coat closet would disappear . . . along with Mickey, slipping away into the mist. I don't know if that was ever proved. With Dora, it's hard to tell which part of his story is myth and which part is truth. He did leave the country in the early seventies to avoid arrest. The mystique surrounding this guy never dies.

I think Dora is known more for what he didn't do than for what he did. He was the kind of guy who would create a situation, like a surf contest in his name, and then not show up. He'd organize all the players in a situation, then sit back and watch the outcome. I think he liked to create chaos.

This happened with a girl Dora liked. As far as I know, it was the closest that he ever came to seriously getting involved with a girl. Dora was going to the Islands, and he asked this friend of his, Frenchy, who was a maître d' at a Hollywood restaurant, for some help in getting this girl on the same airplane. Dora thought it might be nice if he and the girl could spend some time together in Hawaii.

Frenchy spends a lot of energy putting this thing together. Then Dora gets on the airplane and finds this girl sitting in the seat next to him, and he becomes totally enraged. "What are you doing here?" he shouts at her. "You're going to ruin my trip to the Islands!"

When Dora found himself getting into a situation where he might be forced into a closeness with someone, he backed off. He couldn't handle it. He walked off the plane, told Frenchy that he never wanted to speak to him again.

Dora had a funny sense of humor and had a lot of quirks. He'd talk with various phony accents, use his hands to gesture while he was talking or surfing. He cared about things you wouldn't think he'd care about.

130

When I was building his signature board, he'd get fan mail every day. Sometimes we wouldn't see him for a couple weeks. When he'd finally come in the shop, there'd be a stack of fan letters waiting for him. He'd go off in a corner and read every letter, then write a reply to every one of them. He really cared.

He was hired to do stunt riding in the movie *Ride the Wild Surf*. He wasn't a big-wave surfer, but they were paying him and he told them he could do it. The waves were really pumped up that day at Waimea. He didn't like it. Although I hadn't been hired to do stunt riding, I was out there surfing anyway.

Being unfamiliar with Waimea, I could see he was using me for his lineups. At Malibu, he and Johnny Fain had a running battle to see who could come up on the other guy first on a wave and grab his ass or push him off his board. With Fain, it was kind of a fun thing. With anyone else, Dora wasn't kidding. You didn't take off on *his* wave. He'd push you right off or try to cut you off at the knees when he kicked out of the wave.

So here we are at twenty-foot Waimea and I see my chance to get Dora. There is a picture of us that shows me coming down behind him on a twenty-foot wave. What happened was I came rolling up beneath him on my board and grabbed him by the ass. Surprised the hell out of him. All day, I made sure I was always behind him and in the pocket, just to rattle him. In one of his funny accents, he'd say, "Jeez, every time I turn around, you're on my ass! I can't get away from you!"

The funny thing is, these were probably the biggest waves he had ever ridden in his life. That day, he had made a jump from five-or six-foot Malibu waves to twenty-foot Waimea. He was shaky, but he did it. The guy really had ability. I can't think of anyone else who could have made that sort of transition.

Dora's parents were divorced when he was young. His stepfather, Gard Chapin, spent a lot of time with him and introduced him to surfing at San Onofre, but Dora kept his original father's name. When we were kids, Dora once came up with a scheme to burn down the shack at San Onofre. That beach shack is famous and has been there since Day One. Gard Chapin was one of the early San Onofre surfers and Dora wanted to rattle all those old-timers. He had the thing all figured out. He was going to take incendiary bombs and come down the trail by the cliff, burn the thing down, then paint swastikas on the trash cans and outhouses. Of course, he never carried out the plan.

131

The ad campaign we worked up for Dora's board reveals a lot about Dora. He positioned himself as the No. 1 all-around surfer in the world, the No. 1 Cat. Duke Boyd helped work up the ad campaign. Duke was a good friend who had also founded the tremendously successful clothing company Hang Ten International, and thereby earned himself a place in surf history as the father of modern surfwear.

In the first ad, we didn't even mention Dora's name. The ad shows an ocelot sitting on top of a board that's covered by a gold cloth. I'm standing in the background. The heading simply says, "Da Cat is king." The ad copy reads, "Greg Noll overlooks what represents a first, a completely new evolution in the surfing world. Under gold silk cloth lies a surfboard designed, tested and proven by a rider whom many big name and influential surfers refer to as the best all-around surfer in the world . . . the #1 CAT . . . This board, like its name-sake and designer, is controversial in appearance and in the unique, different way it rides."

The next ad said, "Da Cat is coming," and told more about the board and revealed that Dora was the Cat behind it all. So far, we hadn't sold or really manufactured anything, but we had sure built up suspense.

We certainly weren't advertising geniuses, but the campaign worked—for a couple of years, in fact. It worked mainly because Dora played off the mystique that had already built up around him. As though he were the last of the pure surfers in the world and he wasn't going to sell his soul to anyone.

Dora wrote most of the ad copy. I edited it, sometimes toned it down a bit, because Dora tended to get a little radical. After all, I was in the business of selling surfboards, and trying to do it in some manner that made a few bucks and at the same time wasn't a total cartoon.

Other surfboard manufacturers told us that when the new issue of *Surfer* arrived, the first thing they'd do is look to see who Greg and Mickey were screwing over this time, before they looked at their own ads. When you capture your competitors' imaginations to that extent, you know your advertising campaign is working.

Dora did command some respect in the surfing world, and the Cat was one of the most, if not *the* most successful surfboard models during that time period, especially on the East Coast. The farther away from Malibu, the bigger the Dora mystique grew. We couldn't make the boards fast enough for our East Coast dealers. We were getting the outrageous price of a hundred and seventy-five dollars per board at a time when most boards were going for around a hundred and twenty dollars. The more Dora insulted people in the ads, the more they wanted to buy the board. So we just kept insulting them and they kept giving us their money. I never understood how that worked, but we had a good time with it.

Da Cat board was shorter, wider and lighter than conventionally shaped boards of that time. The nose section was dished out, resulting in a thin profile that made turning easier and quicker. For stability, we made the fin deeper and thin at the base for more flexibility. At one time, our shop had sixty-four people turning out over two hundreds boards a week—da Cat and other models—during the summer months. This was during the mid to late sixties. The heydays. The East Coast was blown wide open by then. We had sixty-three dealers on the East Coast at the time. Hobie did even a bigger business. I think Dewey Weber and I were fighting for the second spot.

Other Recollections

BEVERLY

You just had to walk on eggs around Dora. He was always suspicious of anything and everything you said or did. On guard all the time. After he would deal with Greg, Mickey would come over to my desk and stand there, twitching. He had a lot of body movement, especially in his shoulders. He'd say, "What's going on?" It was almost as though he wanted to trust somebody to tell him that everything was O.K.

Once I gave him a birthday card. He was so taken aback that, to this day, I have not forgotten the expression on that man's face. He couldn't figure out why anyone would want to give him a birthday card. He liked it, but he couldn't figure it out.

Other Recollections

DUKE BOYD

I was running a sort of backyard ad agency at the time, and helped out several of my friends who were in the surf business, including Hobie, Bing, the Meistrell brothers and Greg.

Greg and I were shooting the breeze one day when he mentioned a new "secret project" that he and Dora had come up with. They hadn't yet designed the board, so the whole idea revolved around doing a campaign without a product, and building suspense by announcing its coming.

This wasn't your normal surfboard ad campaign. There were a few guys in the surf business who were good at drumming up grassroots interest, much like you see in today's advertising. Greg was one of them. He was a future thinker, in terms of creativity and ability to direct his advertising at the youth market. Other innovative surfers and creative advertisers from that time include Hobie Alter, Dewey Weber, Bing Copeland, Don Hansen and the partners who started G. & S., Larry Gordon and Floyd Smith. There was some hardcore competition among these guys. They continually checked out each other's ads and tried to outdo each other. In so doing, they created an industry and attitude that still survives today, bigger than ever.

The surf industry has changed a lot since Greg's time. The computer-oriented surfer of today doesn't have a pioneer, vagabond, search-for-the-perfect-wave attitude. Instead of stouthearted men looking for surf, today you have young kids looking for money.

Greg and a few other big-wave surfers from that time pioneered the "when men were men" surf era. They discovered the surf spots, established the lineups and made it easier for future surfing generations. For that, they were respected and very often held in awe.

Greg wasn't respected that much in his own town—after all, he had grown up there and everyone knew his underwear was dirty. But outside the South Bay, Greg enjoyed a major reputation as Da Bull, who rode Waimea better than anyone and who built boards that proved it.

In my opinion, the best ad in the entire series was the one called "Da Cat's Theory of Evolution." The ad showed the various stages of the evolution of the surfer, using apes and primitive humans as models, but obviously referring to different surfers of the time, from Johnny Fain to the gang known as the Dana Point Mafia. Of course, Dora placed himself at the top of the evolutionary cycle as a model of the "peak of perfection . . . plus more advanced knowledge and ability."

There's another ad that shows Dora sitting on an overturned trash can. The trash is spilling out. If you look closely, you can see his trophy from the '66 Duke Kahanamoku Invitational sitting there in the trash. Dora hated the idea of contests—they were part of the commercialization that he didn't like—but I think he participated in the Duke Invitational to show everybody that he could do it. Like, it was no big deal to be in a contest. He placed and received a trophy.

The ad reads: "Getting ready to bury this junk with all the rest of the trashy rot that keeps bugging me! Scrap metal tokenism as a grubby little payoff to keep me in line and my mouth shut. Such outside pressures will never succeed in making me a lap dog for the entrenched controlling interests who have turned our once great individualistic sport into a mushy, soggy cartoon."

That same year, Dora also competed in an invitational contest held at Malibu. He made the finals. To illustrate his contempt for the commercialization of surfing, he rode a wave past the judge's stand, bent over and dropped his trunks.

Dora even insulted potential customers: "My name is on da Cat and I have to keep it in the right hands. I don't want some acne stricken adolescent in Pratt Falls, Iowa, using da Cat for a car ornament or some show biz creep in the Malibu Colony using da Cat as a coffee table. Da Cat is too pure and sensitive for the clumsy touch of the occasional pseudo surfer."

I have to admit that I shared many of Dora's views about the commercialization of the sport. The ad campaign brought out some conflicting feelings in me. I was, first and foremost, a surfer. But I also was in the business of selling boards. My business allowed me the freedom to surf, and how well I surfed became a great factor in how many surfboards I sold. I thought I could always keep the two separate, but it was getting harder and harder to do so. By the late sixties, a lot of the fun and camaraderie of the early days had been wiped out by the hordes of aspiring surfers and the ever-present click click click of the surf photographers' cameras, followed closely by the lads with their notebooks and pencils.

OUTSIDE PIPELINE, 1964

Phil Edwards was the first to surf Pipeline, in December 1961. Bruce Brown was there to film it and to secure Edwards' place in surf history. Because Pipeline is such a dangerous, treacherous break, it was one of the last big spots on the North Shore to be broken. Pipeline breaks close in on an inside reef, which makes it nice for spectators and photographers on shore. The wave is fast and wild—it often leaps up in size while you're riding it—with a tubular break that sometimes covers you then spits you out in a spray of water. The worst part is the wave's chasmlike drop into shallow water, where you can get smashed and ripped up on coral heads and lava rocks when you wipe out. Since that day in '61, Pipeline has been ridden and conquered many times, but it's still a spot reserved for more experienced surfers. A contest called the Pipeline Masters is held there every year. Only the best surfers are invited to participate.

Phil Edwards is the guy who tagged me with the nickname Da Bull. One time, when we were at Pipeline, he accused me of being bullheaded because I knew I was going to get wiped out on this one wave, and instead of ejecting like I should have, I just squatted down and got eaten alive. Afterwards, Phil said, "You bullheaded sonofabitch, I think I'll just call you Da Bull from now on." The name stuck.

In all the years I've been going to Hawaii, I've only seen the far Outside Pipeline reef break a few times. It's a rare, white-elephant break. Everything has got to be just right for it to work. The swell has to be really clean and the direction absolutely precise to hit those outside reefs.

I'm talking way outside. First, there's Inside Pipeline, where Phil Edwards was the first to ride and where everyone surfs today. The contests are also held there. Several hundred yards beyond that is a place called Outside Pipeline, which sometimes breaks when Inside Pipeline gets big and nasty. But this isn't the outside reef I'm talking about. Hell, the thing I rode broke on a reef almost a mile out, on the edge of the blue water.

It happened on a day in November 1964. Waimea was breaking straight across, Sunset was unsurfable and Inside Pipeline was a mess. There's a picture from that day that shows me standing on shore, with my arm around my board, watching Pipeline break. It was used as a poster for the movie *Big Wednesday*. What many people don't realize is that the wave in the picture is just shorebreak.

It took Mike and me over an hour just to get out. When we were down near the water, we couldn't see what was going on outside because the shorebreak was so big. So Ricky Grigg spotted for us, up on the beach. I knew I could trust Ricky's judgment. He stayed up high and gave us a sign whenever he thought we should go for it.

To get out, we had to get past this bitch of a shorebreak and through a strong lateral current. After watching it for a while, we noticed that there was one spot where an incoming current hit the lateral current and formed a saddle, a slot where we might be able to take advantage of the current and shoot through the shorebreak. Trouble was, we had to start about three hundred yards up from this spot and drift along with the current, timing it just right so that we'd be sucked out through the slot rather than dumped back on the sand.

We got dumped at least four times before we made it out. We had started fairly early in the morning and ended up spending over eight hours in the water.

When we got outside to that far reef, there were no lineups, nothing to indicate what our position should be. Only four sets broke out there all day. We'd watch a wave break, then paddle like hell to get as close to the whitewater as possible, to determine our lineups. The next wave would break maybe a quarter of a mile away, so we'd paddle hard to get there before the whitewater subsided and establish another point of reference. Then we'd sit there for a couple of hours until another set came along and we'd go through the same routine until we felt we'd tightened up on the lineups.

There were six to eight waves in each set. The sun hit the face of these long walls that faded out towards Waimea Bay and made them breathtakingly beautiful. It was a surreal day. I was so mesmerized I'd stop paddling just to watch one of those beautiful waves move through. They were like pure, liquid energy. Then I'd jerk myself back into reality and say, "You'd better wake up, Pal. If this thing breaks on you, you might end up sucking suds."

The outside wave was still one hell of a tube, like Inside Pipeline. But unlike Inside Pipeline, it also was a long, long wall. Mike and I chugged up and over these waves on our boards, feeling like tiny freighters, dwarfed by the huge seas. Now and then we'd paddle for one. They were almost impossible to get into. They were so big and moving with such speed that we couldn't paddle fast enough to get down the face of the wave. You really had to windmill to have even a prayer of catching one.

To establish our lineups we worked off Kaena Point and back up on the hill behind Pupukea, taking three or four azimuths, until we finally got our lineups in late afternoon, just as this one particular wave came through. It was the only wave I caught that whole day, and it's permanently etched in my memory.

In a twenty-five-foot wave at Waimea, the shoulder drops off. The wave I caught at Outside Pipeline that day walled up twenty-five-feet high about half a mile in front of me. It broke to the left, so I was riding with my back to the wave, goofyfoot, and it was a god-awful uneasy feeling. Instead of getting smaller as I rode it, the sonofabitch grew on me. It got bigger and bigger, and I started going faster and faster, until I was absolutely locked into it. I felt like I was on a spaceship racing into a void. At first, I could hear my board chattering across the face of the wave in a constant rhythm. As my speed increased, the chattering noise became less frequent. Suddenly there was no noise. For about fifteen or twenty feet, I was airborne. Then I literally was blown off my board.

When I hit and went underwater, I thought I was going to drown. I got pounded good before I popped up and started sweating the next wave. It was a big one, too. I saw Mike paddling for it, but he had a shorter board than mine and couldn't get into it.

Other Recollections

MIKE STANGE

It was heart-wrenching to watch Greg catch that wave, because I'd spent all day out there with him. I knew he had probably wiped out and then headed inside. I didn't want to sit out there and wait another three hours for the next set, so in desperation I decided to paddle to the inside reef.

Inside Pipeline is unique in the way it breaks in shallow water. There's a lot of water in the waves, and it moves incredibly fast, bottom to top. When the wave breaks, it snaps like a peal of thunder. It comes over you in a tube and traps wind. You hear and feel all these sensations: the snap, the roar of the moving water, the wind blowing out of the tube. Sometimes, the wind actually helps you by blowing you through the wave.

So I paddled in and took off on a wave. I was only halfway down when it sucked me right back up to the top and threw me over the falls. I hit so hard that when I came up, I wasn't seeing double, I was seeing triple! I was standing in waist-deep water and I saw Greg come running off the beach toward me with a real concerned look on his face. He figured I was going to get ground up on the lava rocks and coral. I was lucky that I didn't.

Other Recollections

BUD BROWNE
Surf Photographer and Movie Producer

I filmed Greg riding that wave at Outside Pipeline. At that time, I lived in a house right at Pipeline, so I could see Greg and Mike Stange on the beach, trying to find a way out through the shorebreak. It was a cloudy, rainy day with very stormy, choppy conditions. By the time they got out, it was afternoon, and the waves were in shadow.

Greg and Mike were the only ones out. Greg waited outside, as he usually did, for a big one. And he got it. It was the most thrilling ride I've ever seen. I used a twelve-inch lens and caught the wave and Greg on it just right. That wave was so fast and powerful, it finally just blasted Greg right off his board. The ride appeared in my movie *Locked In,* and as a clip it's been featured in several surf films since.

Greg had a reputation for taking off on the biggest waves. He looked reckless, with his striped trunks and aggressive maneuvers. Whether he made the wave or wiped out didn't seem to matter to Greg. I think he enjoyed the wipeouts as much as the rides.

RICKY GRIGG

Greg's ride at Outside Pipeline was probably the most exciting ride I have ever seen on film. I say "on film" because you could see it better than from where we were on shore that day. In the film you see the wave get bigger and bigger and bigger . . . it grew because the wave was funneling in, the energy was coming at him and building into the wave as he rode it. It reached a point where the wave was too large for a board that long and a human being to ride it, and it catapulted. You could see the board begin to rise on the wave at that point. The board could not go down the face of the wave as fast as the water was coming up the face.

That's when Greg's body went flying through the air. The wave had to have been twenty-five feet. It was a twenty-foot takeoff. In the movie, it was shown in super slow motion. Every frame was like the agony and the ecstasy opening of "Wide World of Sports," where the guy gets wiped out on the ski jump.

A guy has to get over some real fears to get to the point where the decision to either go or not go becomes automatic. You have to decide how much you're willing to risk, how much you're willing to give up. Your life, maybe? It depends on how badly you want that wave.

The day that Mike and I planned to ride Outside Pipeline, there was a guy running around on the beach like a puppy dog while we were checking out the surf. He had been in the Islands for a month or so, and by God, he was determined to ride some big waves.

He followed us out through the slot, talking himself into it all the way. We heard him saying, "O.K., I'm O.K. I gotta ride one of these things, I'm right behind you guys." Somehow, he got outside and then those sets started to pump up. It's an awesome sight. Until you've become conditioned to it, it can mess up your mind. They come from about a mile away. You can see the crest of the wave begin to feather in the wind and hear the thunder as they roll nearer. Well, this guy sees these big

140

buggers coming at us and he says, "Holy shit, you guys are crazy! I'm gettin' outta here!"

The difference between that type of guy and an experienced big-wave rider is that the experienced rider has made all the right decisions before going out. This other guy is going to grab his board and jump into the water without much thought. That day at Outside Pipeline, Mike and I sat there and looked at the thing for a couple of hours before we went into the water. We took soupline marks, checked the direction of the current, put all these things together and went out with a plan. A set breaks, you paddle like hell towards the whitewater, then hit your lineups. The next set breaks out a little farther. You keep working and finally you get those lineups tightened up to where you think that thing is going to be, based on previous sets that have broken or boils that appear over shallow spots. This is what you do on uncovered ground.

Since no one had surfed that far offshore from Pipeline before, we didn't know where the reefs were located. Mike and I sat for several hours in perfectly blue water on the lineups we had figured before a set finally came and broke there. You have to be able to do that, to stick by your decision and sit there for three hours or as long as it takes, knowing, "By God, one broke here. I paddled in on the soupline and one broke and the surf's still big. Another one's got to break here."

LINEUPS AND BREAKS

Lineups are heavy-duty deals in big surf. If you don't have a reference point that tells you where a wave is going to break, you'll never catch a wave. Instead it'll end up catching you. Today, at every surf spot on the North Shore, except for a few of the outside breaks, the lineups are already established. When we first started exploring the North Shore, we had to figure out the lineups whenever we surfed a new spot.

Everybody uses everybody else's lineups. Even so, some styles lend themselves to different lineups. I was a fairly strong paddler, so I could come from way outside to catch a wave. I'd work on that particular aspect of my style so that I could be farther back, coming from the inside of the break. Consequently, a long board, fast paddling and taking off on the wave early put me in a certain lineup. A guy like Ricky Grigg, with a paddling style of a quick scratch and you're up, has to position himself differently.

To surf Big Waimea, you've got to have dead-fast faith in your lineups. You base your decisions on what you know is going to happen, not on what looks like is going to happen. If you go by what looks like is going to happen—such as, it looks like the wave is going to close out—you won't take off and you'll miss the ride of your life.

An accomplished big-wave rider knows a lot about the ocean and the bottom conditions. Sometimes, during the summer, I would go diving at Waimea or Sunset for the sole purpose of checking the reefs and bottom structure. It's very interesting to go out at one of these places in the summer, when the surf is as flat as a swimming pool. You paddle out on your board, check your lineups—O.K., there's where I was sitting—then dive straight down. You find a reef directly under you, and that's why the

142

wave broke there. When you've been away from the North Shore during the off-season, it's very reassuring to paddle out and sit on your lineups again. At first, you're always a little unsure of where you are. Then a set comes through that leaves you sitting on a boil. A big boil, maybe three or four times the size of an average living room. Then you know you're right on target.

After Mike and I surfed Outside Pipeline that one day, we knew we might have been faced with a different set of lineups had we gone out the next day. There are so many reefs out there that each time the place breaks it's likely to break a little different than the last time. On any particular day, if the swell direction changes even two degrees, you could end up surfing a quarter of a mile from where you were the day before. You sometimes have to make up lineups as you go.

Waimea is different. Waimea has a basic swell that comes through and changes one direction or the other. All you do is adjust accordingly. When we first paddled out at Waimea, with all the legends and taboos hanging over us like a storm cloud, what was part of our lineup? A cross on a church steeple, of all things. We expected the clouds to part and a voice to boom down upon us, "Thou hast tred on sacred ground. Thou shalt die." It was a pretty heavy deal for those of us who were there the first time around.

All that mystery is gone now. The guys who surf Waimea Bay today have a historical base to draw upon. I doubt if many of them ever give a second thought to the mystery, the legends, the aura that once surrounded Waimea. Now that I've come to terms with the fact that my time at Waimea has come and gone, I can finally take satisfaction in knowing that I helped pave the way for future generations of surfers. As kids at Manhattan Beach Pier, all Bing and I had to go on were surfers on heavy redwood boards. Now, with years of evolution in board design and surfing style behind them, kids can start out at a much higher level.

When you get on a wave at Makaha, you can look across the face of that wave and see a long wall ahead of you. In comparison to Makaha, Waimea is a peak break. But not a peak like Sunset. Waimea has more of a wall to it when it gets big, when the swell direction is from the Sunset side. With enough size and wind on it in the afternoon, there are times when the damn thing can throw up a wall that looks straight across the Bay. One long wall of water.

At times like that, after you get past the critical area, you pass a hard reef that creates a big boil. The water goes from around twenty feet deep to about thirty-five feet or deeper off the back side of that boil. At this point, if the wave is starting to break half a block in front of you, you know it means either a swim or a ride in the whitewater. But if you can get into the wave, straighten out and blow past that boil far enough, you can get away with murder by dropping down on your board, sinking your fingers into the rails and belly-sliding through the wave. As the wave passes across that deep spot, it backs off, and instead of crushing you under tons of whitewater, it covers you with a pile of soup that turns to feathers. From a photographer's point of view, when a surfer comes flying out of that soup, it looks impossible. I loved the feeling of getting covered up with tons of whitewater and still maintaining control. But, I knew I had to be smokin' off that wave and hit that boil just right to make it all work.

Waimea's my all-time favorite spot. For a period of time on the face of God's earth, I would like to think that there were certain days that Waimea was mine. Ken Bradshaw, Roger Erickson or any one of the other greats who surf there regularly nowadays might find a time that's his, too. But no one ever owns Waimea forever.

Other Recollections

PETER COLE

The past few years, I've been surfing at Makaha because it's been such a zoo at Waimea. But I can't seem to get used to that bowl at Makaha. I've never been able to get across the wave there. You get used to riding the North Shore, which is all peaks. At Makaha, you're coming off the bottom and you forget to trim up at the halfway point.

The first day I ever went out at Sunset Beach, in the late fifties, I had seventeen swims. That has to be some sort of record. Every wave was a killer. I used a Robertson-Sweet Malibu board that didn't even hold in on a two-foot wave at Malibu. Now here I was, trying to ride Sunset Beach with it. Ricky Grigg was with me. He had a bump board made by Velzy. Talk about bad equipment—every time we took off, it was a swim. Years later, when José Angel and I would surf together, our wives would watch us from the beach and point to where our boards had washed in. That was before leashes were used, and guys were swimming in all over the place. My wife, Sally, has been going again to watch Peter junior, but now there's only one guy swimming in for his board: me. Every time I swim in at Sunset, I enjoy it. I try to bodysurf in, and roll with the whitewater.

Most of the other surfers from my day who are still surfing now use leashes on their boards. Flippy Hoffman must have one leg longer than the other. He has this big-wave board that weighs about 40 pounds that he once took out at Waimea with a leash. I saw it drag him into the beach. I have a nine-foot, six-inch noserider, but the board I ride at Sunset Beach is a ten-ten. Kenny Bradshaw makes my boards now. For Waimea, I have a twelve-foot board that weighs thirty-eight pounds. Like Greg, I always have used wide boards. Mine are twenty-four inches wide. And too heavy for a leash.

The guys surfing today are better—every generation improves on the one before—but I don't know if they have as much fun as we did in the fifties and early sixties. The first time I met Henry and Buff was when I was driving over to the North Shore with a few other surfers—Chubby Mitchell, Kimo Hollinger and Paul Gebauer. It was my first month in the Islands and I could not believe how much fun it was. Buff and Henry gave me my first, and last, taste of swipe. It tasted sweet, good. After two glasses of that stuff, my mouth got numb and I passed out. Nobody told me it was pure alcohol. I used to call Buff to get a surf report on Makaha. He'd tell me, "Ah, the waves are beautiful, ten to twelve feet." I'd drive over—nothing. Not a wave in sight. "Where are the waves, Buff?" He'd say, "Nice, you come keep me company, Peter."

What keeps Ricky Grigg and I going out there is that surfing has not been a regular thing for us. We surf after work and on weekends. Georgie Downing is still a regular at Makaha, and he goes out at Laniakea with me. There aren't too many of us from the old days still out there. We're not as aggressive as we used to be. The waves look bigger now, you know!

Today's big-wave riders aren't very patient. The big waves pass them by while they're busy taking off on everything else. Here I am, in my late fifties, and I'm the only one left sitting on the lineups. Greg and I were good at waiting. We knew if we were going to catch a big wave we had to wait. The last time I saw Greg I said to him, "Aren't you glad we're as old as we are? We had the best of it."

RICKY GRIGG

I think Greg and I rode big waves for different reasons. We provided a lot of inspiration to each other, but to me, from the very beginning, riding a big wave was a matter of curiosity. It was beautiful, magnetic. I was drawn into it almost involuntarily. I had to go out there and get into it.

I remember on January 10, 1953, when Rincon was breaking fifteen to twenty feet, I didn't even think twice about going out. It was so beautiful that I just found myself doing it. It wasn't a fearsome thing. Those fabulously huge waves were so majestic, wrapping around that point. You could paddle outside, watch and study them. That's when I got hooked. Then we all started riding really big waves and it became competitive. You got damn scared at times. You got so scared you needed each other to do what you were doing. I've been real scared at Waimea, whereas on the Mainland I was never scared. I've taken off on waves at Waimea that I probably wouldn't have, had Greg Noll not been watching.

KEN BRADSHAW
Big-Wave Surfer, Surfboard Shaper

I grew up in Texas. The first time I went surfing, my mother took me and my sister and some of our friends to the Gulf, and we rented Greg Noll surfboards. It didn't take me long to realize that I'd have to go somewhere else to get bigger surf. In 1969, after high school, I left Texas and headed for California. By 1971 I was in Hawaii. The next year, Jeff Blears introduced me to George Downing. George became my mentor and shaped my first Hawaiian boards. A set of four.

When Waimea breaks under eighteen feet, it gets crowded and dangerous. That's when guys who want to say that they've surfed Waimea go out. They sit in the bowl area for a fifteen-foot wave and end up in everyone's way when a set comes through. At eighteen to twenty feet, that second reef starts to pump and the crowd splits up. You get maybe twenty guys hustling for it. The first set that hits twenty-five feet, that's it. You're suddenly down to six or eight guys. It's that first big dark one that clears it out real fast.

I first surfed Big Waimea in '73. Today there's a pack of guys who regularly surf it when it's big, including Derek Doerner, Michael Ho, Johnny Boy Gomes, Tony Moniz, Mark Foo, Roger Erickson and myself. Twenty-five years ago, that pack might have been Greg Noll, Mike Stange, Peter Cole, Ricky Grigg, José Angel, Buzzy Trent, George Downing. The crowds on the beach may have increased, but the number of guys in the water on a big day has stayed about the same.

Several years ago, when I'd be out at Waimea on big days with my friend Eddie Aikau, he'd try to get me to take off with him on some giant waves that looked to me like close-outs. Eddie would say, "Come on, Brudda Brad, come on, Brudda Brad," and I'd look at that thing and it would be feathering all the way down the line. I remember three different occasions where I went ahead and followed Eddie, followed the lineups, instead of thinking about what that wave looked like. We just took off. I found myself at the bottom, looking up at the top of this monster about to cave in on me, looking at it all the way down the face about to fold over on me. Then it suddenly backed off at that deep spot and I made it through. It's unreal when you get it like that.

I've been surfing the outer reefs for a little over ten years. I won't go out there unless it's breaking big. It takes a long time to paddle out and establish some sort of lineup. I go out there when there's a contest on at Waimea or when I decide to give up Waimea for a day. The outside reefs are a neat challenge, but there is no wave in the world that is as efficient as Waimea. Efficient, because it breaks right there on the lineups every time. If you're in position, you can just hop on wave after wave after wave. To surf an outside reef, you have to be there when it breaks, which is rare to begin with.

When guys talk about riding Outside Pipeline today, they're talking about the second reef. The wave that Greg Noll caught at Outside Pipeline in November of '64 broke on the third reef. I've been out there, but I've never ridden it. The reef is there, and it drops off into the deep blue. There's no bottom in sight.

I come from the same school of thought that Greg does. I believe that surfing should be done exactly as it was meant to be done: man versus the ocean. The surfer goes out and faces his personal challenge, and on his own, he either succeeds or fails.

I'm also into the rush you get from dropping into a monster at Big Waimea. You go from zero to sixty in a snap, free-falling part of the way. When you go over the edge of a twenty-five-foot wave, your brain speeds up to take it all in and then it all actually seems to unfold in slow motion. You see the boils, the bumps, the ridges, the different colors in the water. You see every little thing. The preparation and paddling, the excitement and enormousness of it all come into focus and then you're just doing it. Flying down the face of the wave.

I sometimes paddle out, way beyond shore, beyond the outside reefs, just to sit out on the ocean. There is great truth to be learned from the ocean. Every year, I learn something more about myself, just from being out there.

MARS, THE BRINGER OF WAR

One winter during the late sixties, the North Shore was getting bombed by some particularly heavy swells. I knew that it had hit one day and was the beginning of a good, two-to-three-day run of big surf. So I caught the red-eye flight out of Los Angeles and planned to be in the water the following morning.

As the plane started its approach into Honolulu airport, I was listening to music on the headset and looking out the window at the lights of Waikiki and Honolulu below. I could feel my adrenalin building. I was about thirty years old. My confidence had never been better. At some point in the life of big-wave riders, experience begins to contribute as much as physical strength. That day at Big Makaha, I was at the height of my confidence, but not as physically fit as I was this day, flying into Oahu for another winter session.

I started turning the channels and hit the classical music station just as it began playing a selection from "The Planets" by Gustav Holst. I don't know if the music matched my mood or if my mood was heightened by the music, but I suddenly felt like a warrior being carried into battle on the wings of an eagle.

I looked out the window and listened to this incredible symphony as we banked over Honolulu, and I was overwhelmed by the feeling that there wasn't a wave that God could produce that I couldn't ride. I visualized men going into battle in the days of King Arthur, not knowing if they would live or die, but feeling supremely confident and alive, full of adrenalin and raw enthusiasm.

When I stepped off that plane and that warm Island air hit me, I had all the goddamned confidence of a rhinoceros. I think if Kaena Point had

149

been breaking forty foot that night, I'd have gone out and ridden it in the dark. It was a sort of blind, stupid feeling, one of those moments that more than likely nobody else would understand, so I never told anyone about it.

From the very beginning, it has always been a joy to me to ride a bigger wave. At one time, a six-foot wave was pretty terrifying. Then, I got comfortable at that stage and an eight-foot wave was intimidating. And then a ten-foot wave challenged me, and so on. At one point, I was as comfortable riding twenty-foot waves as I had been riding six-footers.

And the thrill was always there. Surfing is like an addiction. You always need more size to satisfy you. I was comfortable with twenty-foot waves, but they weren't enough. I think what finally happened was that I realized, that day at Big Makaha, how the addiction was bordering on insanity. At some point, a guy has to ask himself, "Are you going to slip over the goddamn edge or are you going to keep this thing in perspective?"

There is a physical dimension in surfing that a human being cannot exceed. I hit that wall plenty of times, with all the crazy things I tried to do. After that day at Makaha, I realized that I was trying to exceed a physical limitation. I wasn't using good sense.

There were times, on some of the bigger waves—twenty-five-foot or bigger—when I was held under so long that I would begin to black out as I came up to surface. The first time this ever happened, I thought, "Christ, I almost drowned!" But even that got to the point where I was pushing the limit so hard that it became a somewhat acceptable routine to burst to the surface and have so little oxygen left that I'd be in a state of actually passing out. I'd take in air, see stars and feel the very early stages of unconsciousness. How much farther can you push it than that? When I realized how insane this was getting, I decided that I really didn't want to find out. I figured, somewhere along the line, it's going to be all black and the light just isn't gonna come back.

Lots of people have brought up the idea that riding big waves is a death wish. I never thought of it as that. But a few times, when I'd get my butt kicked really good on a big wave and really get whipped around underwater, I'd start laughing. Laughing on the bottom, waiting for the wave to let me go.

Sometimes I'd go out at Sunset on a fifteen-foot day and just get blasted off my board. I'd get ripped sideways underwater, feel like my

150

arms were being torn out of their sockets, and I'd start giggling. Even getting wiped out was fun.

There would be times when I'd come up after a bad wipeout and guys would be paddling out and see me, giggling, or with a smile on my face. They'd say, "What the hell are you smiling at?" I was always too embarrassed to admit that I enjoyed it. Maybe a guy gets himself into a state of being where he feels invincible. I don't think that's a death wish. I see it as just living close to the edge. Don't get me wrong. There were plenty of times when I took a good-old-fashioned ass-bashing and it was no fun.

At times, getting wiped out was actually a sort of controlled feeling. I knew I had control, even though I was getting slapped around. There were times at Sunset when it was so pretty underwater. I would dive deep under a breaking wave, dive into blue water, then turn over and open my eyes to watch the sunlight slicing through the turbulent whitewater, coming at me like a hurricane of light.

THE NEXT WAVE

I was never a great waterman like Mike Bright or Peter Cole. I think it was more mental conditioning that got me through big waves. Physical conditioning was almost secondary.

Nevertheless, there is a physical barrier that stops you. At a certain point, a wave gets so big and moves so fast that it's a killer. A big-wave surfer doesn't get many chances to go after a wave that's just skirting the edge of being a killer. In a fifteen-to-twenty-year time period, there are only a couple of days that show themselves like that day at Big Makaha in '69. At that time, you have to be mentally prepared to make a decision that may cost you the farm.

When you get up in the neighborhood of waves twenty feet and over, there's also another element to consider, and that's the force and speed of the wave. Swells move in the open ocean at about thirty-five miles per hour. As they near shore, or the reef where they're going to break, their speed increases. Along with the increase in speed you also get an increase in the force of the wave. When it breaks on you, it can drive you twenty feet underwater, if you're lucky to be in water that deep. So no matter what mental and physical condition a surfer might be in, the wave may be beyond his capabilities. That's why the biggest waves at Waimea, Makaha, Kaena Point and the outside reefs still go unridden.

Every so often a surfer comes along who says he's going to ride Kaena Point when it's breaking forty feet or more. Seems like these guys want to be heroes based on what they say they're going to do, rather than on what they actually do. One of these days somebody will get a boat to take him into a giant wave and a helicopter to take him out, he'll be equipped with oxygen and he'll do it. But it won't be surfing in the true sense.

The true sense means casting aside all the bullshit and paddling out there on your own board, paddling into the wave under your own steam, riding the damn thing and then getting out of there on your own.

Other Recollections

RICKY GRIGG

There is a wave off an outside reef that I saw that feathers in about eighty feet of water. You'd have to pull a surfer into a wave fifty feet or bigger, because he wouldn't have any chance in the world of being in the right spot at the right time. It's too tenuous. So you pull him in, he rides the face of the wave, and it's not as dangerous as Big Makaha or Big Waimea, but it will be done and it will be photographed and it will look bigger, but it won't be as hairy. I think guys will even do it on sailboards. They will ride sixty-foot waves on sailboards out in deep, deep water where it's safe and they can sail away from the wave.

There are a lot of guys who feel that the waves on the North Shore were bigger in the old days, especially at Waimea. Some people think this is due to the pirating of sand from the beach at Waimea Bay for construction of the Ala Moana shopping mall outside Honolulu. But that had very little to do with what happened to the waves. If you look at the oceanography of the situation, there were some big storms that changed the amount of sand in the bay. During 1982 to 1984, there were a lot of swells from the west that took sand from offshore and pushed it shoreward, built more wall into the Bay and made it shallower. So when the waves came in, they'd hit the reef, jack up and just throw forward in a big, catapulting, top-to-bottom, pointy sort of wave that didn't get as big as Big Waimea usually does.

Now it's changing again. Everything is always changing. Most people don't live long enough to experience several different cycles and to see how the world naturally changes. For example, eighteen thousand years ago, the sea level off Waikiki was four hundred feet lower than it is today.

153

For some reason, the surfers from Greg's and my generation were more aggressive in riding big waves than they are today. I think the reason is that today's surfers have other interests. The glory is in winning contests and getting endorsements. Before, riding the biggest wave had not been done. Now guys have been doing it for the past twenty-five years. And the waves that are being ridden today are as big as the ones we rode back then.

In '85, there were some thirty-to-thirty-five-foot waves that broke at Waimea and there were guys out in the water. Mark Foo, a well-known big-wave rider, caught one and he got murderously wiped out. He didn't ride it. He nevertheless caught a wave over thirty feet. On February 23, 1985, I was out at Makaha and I have never seen waves like I saw that day. They were at least thirty-five feet. I didn't catch any.

That same day, Waimea was breaking forty feet. Peter Cole called me at work around ten o'clock that morning and said, "Ricky, this is going to be some kind of a day. You've got to leave right now and meet me at Waimea." We met there around twelve-thirty. We stood on the point and watched it peel off, a perfect, ridable forty-foot wave. But if you had paddled out it would have been aloha. There was no way to get back in, because the current was so strong. The shorebreak was halfway out to the break. You would had to have gone through ten big waves just to get out to your lineups.

From the beginning, a lot of us big-wave surfers have had a strong interest in knowing when the surf was coming up. The theory of predicting ocean waves had been developed before World War II by physical oceanographers. During World War II, they had to predict surf conditions on the beaches at Normandy. The call was quite wrong, and thousands of men were lost. Out of these early theories emerged all the theory that we used later to predict surf in Hawaii, to check theory against empirical observations. In this way we learned how to accurately forecast waves and have been doing it pretty routinely since then.

What we've also learned in the last ten or fifteen years is that the crust of the earth is moving about three inches a year toward the northwest. This process is what caused the Hawaiian Islands to form. There is a hot spot, a place like a blowtorch in the earth's mantle where lava has melted the crust, where islands keep forming. Every time a new island is formed, the one that preceded it is moved off the source, the hot spot, to take its place in a long line of islands. Each island takes a million or two million years to form. The first island formed in the chain, Muiji, is seventy million years old, and it's now underwater. What we found in our coral studies is that the coral keeps the islands at sea level. All the islands in the chain north of Gardner are coral. When you get north of Midway and Kiri, to a place called the Darwin Point, coral stops growing at that latitude and the islands drown.

There's a whole series of Hawaiian Islands underwater that used to be where Oahu is today. That's what makes the North Shore unique now as a big-wave spot—it happens to be at just the right latitude and facing just the right angle in its evolution. The storms start up off Kamchatka, in the Aleutians, then they spin up and come across, up the gulf of Alaska. They reach their peak not too far above the Darwin Point and cause swells to hit Oahu at the same point where many other islands once sat.

If you look at this in a larger setting of time, you realize that Oahu's North Shore is just a speck in time. I think that's the closest form of immortality, to experience events in the past and in the future, far beyond your own life, just through what you learn. Then your life just telescopes in all directions, and you come closer to figuring out who you are and how you fit into this whole thing.

SEA MONSTERS, WARRIORS AND WIPEOUTS

A few years ago I started checking out the current surf scene at a trade show in Southern California. I was standing around, talking to a couple of guys, when I felt a strange, magnetic-like pull on my back. It felt so eerie I didn't even want to turn around. I kept talking, but the feeling wouldn't go away.

I finally turned around and saw this stocky, bearded individual standing about ten feet away. He had his arms crossed over his chest and was watching me. He looked familiar. I thought I had seen him surf, but I didn't know his name: All I knew was, that magnetic feeling came from him.

When I finish my conversation, this guy comes walking over to introduce himself. "Hi, I'm Ken Bradshaw. I surf Waimea now and I remember your deal."

We get to talking about lineups and board design and I find that some of his feelings are in line with mine. We come from two different eras, but the battleground hasn't changed and the sea monsters are the same.

Since 1969, other than to my family and a few close friends, I purposely hadn't talked much about Waimea or big surf. But I had a really great talk with Ken. The most interesting guys I've ever known were ones who have actively surfed Waimea. I think that the experience of riding big waves becomes part of you and is recognizable to others who share the experience.

Every big-wave rider I've ever met is a radical individual. Ken

Bradshaw has got the spark. He's intense, he wants it and he's willing to give up something for it if he has to. You have to be that way to ride big waves.

Ken Bradshaw spent many years riding big waves before he got any recognition for it. You have to love what you're doing to go out there and do it when the bleachers are empty. To me that's what surfing is all about.

Other Recollections

KEN BRADSHAW

For years I wondered, "What ever happened to Greg Noll?" I never understood how he could just quit surfing and walk away from it after being so devoted for so many years. It wasn't until I met him and talked to him that I finally understood.

I love and admire the purist side of Greg Noll. In many ways, I share his feelings. But I also live in the competitive and professional world of surfing. As I've become more in touch with the world around me, as I've gotten out of my little sphere of just being a surfer who surfs Sunset Beach and Waimea Bay, I've begun to realize that there's great purpose in the magazines, the books, the TV clips about surfing. There's very little known about the sport. People want and need to hear about the history of our sport and why we've dedicated so much of our lives to it.

In my travels for different sponsors and organizations, I get to talk to lots of kids. When the talk gets off onto the commercial and professional side of surfing, I try to explain to them why I do it and how I found a way to make a living at it. Many of the kids today get all charged up about surfing for all the wrong reasons. They say, "Wow, imagine getting your picture in the magazines and all those chicks." Those are the two things that matter: your picture in the magazine and "chicks." Not the beauty and exhilaration of the sport. Not even the career possibilities in surfing.

The great majority of surfers in the world ride waves four feet and under. This is the part of the surfing world that gets most of the media attention, and this is the population catered to by the surf clothing manufacturers. Big-wave riders are off in another world of their own.

Still, there is a common bond that unites all surfers: the ocean.

Riding big waves is easier today because surfers know it can be done. Greg Noll proved that Waimea Bay could be ridden. He opened the door to the unknown, which has made it easier for me and many other surfers to experience Waimea Bay today. Could I have been able to take my big-wave riding as far as I have without Greg Noll's experience and the experience of his peers to build on? I'm around the same age as Greg was when he stopped riding Waimea. Who knows where the surfers coming up behind me will take big-wave riding?

Other Recollections

RICKY GRIGG

Kenny Bradshaw is one of the few surfers out at Waimea Bay today who does it like we used to, with the same fanatical vigor. The guy claws his way into a wave. He's so strong in the water, so aggressive. There are other guys out there with lots of style, but Kenny has true grit. It's something that comes out of thunder and lightning.

When Kenny is out at Waimea, he dominates the place, physically. The other guys have a difference in attitude. They ride waves with more of an idea of cutting up the face, rather than taking a commanding presence on the wave. They fence with the wave, rather than take it by the horns. These guys are good, some of them are awfully good. You've got to give them credit for doing stuff we could never do.

Most accomplished big-wave riders are in their thirties. It takes a long time to build the experience and, mainly, the judgment required to ride big waves. It builds in you. You get mean!

I think it's great that more surfers today can make a living through something they love doing. I don't think the sport is overcommercialized. The sociology between our time and theirs is different. There are a few guys who have come through the commercial process over the past twenty years or so and still have retained their individuality, such as Nat Young in the late sixties, Mark Richards in the seventies and Ken Bradshaw in the eighties. These guys are so individualistic that nothing can alter their inner beings. The commercialism gives them money and fame, but they emerge from all that when the surf comes up and they go out and show that they are something more.

PETER COLE

A lot of us suffered injuries in the water during wipeouts. Some of us also got it on shore. I'll never forget the time a bunch of us were at Haleiwa shooting off penny rockets and Greg shot me with one, right in the ear. I didn't have very good hearing anyway, so I never could tell how much damage he'd done.

It's funny how you get injured more often in smaller surf. Buffalo and I once were in the hospital together. He had broken his neck and I was in for an eye injury.

Buffalo had been surfing at Makaha and hit the backwash. When he fell, he smashed the cartilage in his neck and was paralyzed from the neck down. He didn't realize it at first. Then he noticed that his hands and legs were just going every which way in the water, out of control. He held his breath, hoping to float to the surface. Wave after wave hit him and literally washed him into shore, where he continued to roll up and down the sand as the waves washed in and out. Finally a couple of guys heard his cries for help and pulled him out of the water. Buff's a real hero to the boys who hang out at Makaha, and they were freaked out. The doctor told Buff he'd never swim or surf again, but he did, and still does. He went through a long rehabilitation.

My eye injury happened when I swam into the fin on my surfboard. Ricky Grigg and I were just goofing around in five-foot surf. We had lost our boards and were swimming in, racing each other. The board was lying there in the water, fin up, and I just swam right into it. I don't get any use out of the eye at all. So here I am, practically blind in both eyes and deaf. Everyone says I'm a menace to the surfers around me because I won't use a leash. I'm afraid I'll get hit with my own board! I can still see well enough to surf. I see color contrast and it's easy to see the waves, but I don't see the surfers. I almost ran over my own son one day when we were surfing Sunset Beach together.

159

RICKY GRIGG

I never saw anyone hit so hard as Greg did during one of his wipeouts at Waimea. He free-fell about fifteen feet straight down and landed on his board. He was only halfway down the face when the whole wave threw forward, buckled and Greg disappeared into a tempest. I have never seen a guy get hit like that. I thought we had lost him then forever, but he made it back to the surface. When you see someone survive that kind of impact, it gives you reassurance that, well, you're going to survive, too.

In '82 I fractured my neck in a wipeout. I free-fell, like Greg did, but I missed my board and went farther out in the air and landed flat on my back. When you're going that fast and land on your back, your head cracks back against your spine, like whiplash. My seventh vertebra was fractured. Luckily, it wasn't a dislocation fracture, so there was no damage to the nerve core. It took a lot of traction and rehabilitation, but I was able to come out of that without being paralyzed. Needless to say, I didn't surf anymore that year.

Another time I got hit in the forearm by my board. At first I didn't know where I was hit. I felt the pain in my back. It took me several minutes to figure it out. Fortunately, it hit on the tissue instead of on the bone and didn't bust my arm. It left a hematoma the size of a grapefruit.

I use a twenty-two-foot leash when I surf Waimea. One of the things that makes the sport so exciting for me is the way the equipment has changed so dramatically. I find it exciting to be out there, still learning, in my fifties. I've been twenty-five feet underwater, out of breath, and pulled myself up on that damn leash a dozen times. Leashes also drag you up as the wave takes your board toward shore. So if you're down deep, you can pull and get pulled up at the same time.

At the end of a good ride, Greg would do this whirly thing with his hand, like Chubby Checker doing the twist. It was classic. After you make a big wave and come out at the end of it, you feel a sense of relief and exhilaration, like, "Whew! Cheated death again!" You feel a tremendous release of tension and anxiety. You put your life on the line and, somehow, you lucked out. You're continually reassured that you can do these things and not die. This gives you confidence that you carry right through your life.

Except with girls. Everything else is a piece of cake. When it comes to girls, it's a whole different ballgame. Buzzy Trent used to say, "Riding a big wave is like riding a great woman." It's equally as exhilarating. A big wave is also like a bucking bronco. Somehow, you shouldn't be on that thing.

Many people don't have any idea how powerful a breaking wave is. You can go to the beach and get knocked over by waist-high shorebreak. Imagine a wall of water the size of a two-story house falling on you. Buzzy Trent was once out in Makaha Point surf when it was breaking twenty feet. He took off on a giant wave and wiped out so bad that when the wave came down on him it snapped his leg like a toothpick. That's raw power.

What you discover out on the ocean is that all the rules everyone makes up are just that: things that people make up. There is nothing fixed, nothing sacred about somebody else's rules. You come back to shore and people try to tell you to do what they think is right. It's not right; it's what someone else has decided. Then you realize that you can change the rules. You can make up better rules for yourself, rules that are based on feelings instead of on power.

Riding big waves teaches you a lot about life, about making commitments. That's an important thing that transfers into the rest of your life, into marriage, friendships. Making a wave is the hard part. Keeping commitments is the hard part.

The worst wipeout I ever experienced was when Ricky and I were surfing Waimea. I got a concussion from hitting my board and I totally blacked out underwater. I had hit the board so hard that my head had left a deep impression in the flat part, between the stringer and the rail. If my head had hit the rail, the hardest part of the board, it would have been aloha. When the board washed up on the beach, strands of my hair were still stuck in the ding.

161

When I came to, I was still underwater. I suddenly realized that I had been unconscious and that I was out of air. Instead of my usual sense of confidence and control, all I felt was nausea and total disorientation. I panicked and started clawing my way to the surface. Luckily, I headed the right way. Sometimes, you get so disoriented, you hit the bottom instead.

I broke the surface just as another wave hit and pounded me back under the water. I gulped more water than air, and almost blacked out again, waiting for the turbulence to release me. It was all I could do to keep my wits about me, to fight the panic. I had worked myself up to the point where I could hold my breath for three minutes, but I'd exceeded my limit this time. I felt doomed.

I guess God was granting reprieves that day. The doctor who treated my concussion told me that the reason I didn't drown when I was unconscious probably was because I had held my breath underwater for so long and so many times that it had become a natural reflex.

Other Recollections

MIKE STANGE

If you look at all the pictures from our era that were taken at Waimea Bay, you'll see who is on the biggest and the most waves: Greg Noll. He's the Babe Ruth of surfing.

Greg and I have been best pals since we lived in the Islands in '54. Between '54 and '65 I was able to ride a few fairly big waves—some of them with Greg. Skin diving, swimming and water polo are what held me together in big surf. I was in good shape, but I never considered myself to be a great surfer. I worked as a lifeguard from 1953 to 1983. When I'd had enough of the whole beach scene, I retired and moved to Northern California with Mazie, my lifelong companion. Surfing big waves was the high point of my youth. Mazie has become the high point of my middle and, hopefully, later years.

A few years ago, I went back to that spot near Wahiawa that looks out over Haleiwa and that same feeling of awe that I had felt the first time we surfed the North Shore came back to me. That whole time we spent in the Islands in the fifties was such an adventure. For me it was a whole new world. We closed out an era. Now I'm proud that I followed Greg to what seemed like the end of the world.

Although I did well in paddling contests when I was younger, I never entered many surfing contests. In my day, there were no contests held at Waimea. Most were held in small surf, except for the Duke Kahanamoku Invitational, which was one of the forerunners of the pro circuit. The Duke was held at Sunset Beach. And there's a world of guys who rode Sunset Beach better than I did. The first Duke Invitational was held in December '65. I was honored to have been selected to surf in several of the contests. One year, when Sunset was breaking big, I placed fourth.

Once I got hooked on riding big waves, I devoted all my energy to that. Lots of guys looked good in smaller surf, they had a lot of control and really performed. That was their niche. When there were big-enough waves and the right conditions all came together, I basically had one thing going for me: I could get my butt down the side of a good-sized wave. That was my niche.

EXOTIC FISH STORIES

I like to catch fish—salmon or steelhead in the river—and I like to raise different varieties of goldfish. My interest in goldfish started with some Japanese friends I met when I was going to high school in Hawaii. Japanese are known for their patience. My friends would squat by a fish pond and stare at it for hours at a time. They might talk a bit about certain fish, but mostly they'd just stare. I spent a great deal of time with these guys and learned a lot about fish. And about patience.

I've kept in touch with one of the guys, Kobiyoshi. He has a strain of fish that he's been developing ever since I was in high school. I have several fish from him, including a Calico Oranda. They're pretty little fish, with exotic head growth and brocaded scales.

I also have a Black Oranda that was smuggled into the country from Red China by a sailor. I bought it from a Chinaman in San Francisco. They're very rare and very tame. I bought a couple of females and they spawned. Now I have a whole family of Black Orandas.

Other Recollections

LAURA

Greg was always looking for beautiful and unusual goldfish. We'd leave Crescent City on a Saturday morning and drive to San Francisco and spend the day, discovering people, usually Chinese, who had gold-fish. We'd walk through the back streets in Chinatown, to little stores where people hardly spoke English, and look at fish. Greg made friends easily with these fellow fish lovers and many times we'd end up in a Chinese tenement building, looking at a Chinaman's personal collection. We'd drive home that same evening and very often spend the rest of the night watching our new fish.

My Veil Tails come from England. What makes them unique, besides their rareness, is their long, veillike tails. About eighteen years ago, I had tried to get some Calico Veil Tails from a guy in England named McMillan, but he didn't want to part with any. In '86, I met a guy from Texas who raised them. I asked him what strain they were from and he told me that he got them from a guy in England named McMillan, who had since died. We traded some of my fish for a few of his Veil Tails. The breeder in Texas has since let his strain go, so I'm now the only Calico Veil Tail breeder I know of here in the U.S.

When we moved to Crescent City, I built several ponds for my fish. It's a beautiful thing to watch them spawn. You wake up on a hot summer morning and see the pond full of color splashes. I keep the males and females isolated until it's time to spawn. The males chase the females around the lily pads, their fins cutting and splashing the surface. The oriental paintings you see of exotic goldfish are of them spawning. The male comes up behind the female and nudges her, chases her until she lays her eggs, usually on water hyacinth. In his excitement the male passes over the eggs and fertilizes them. I've seen four or five males chase one female. They create a rainbow of colors in the pond.

I also hand-spawn some of my fish to make sure I'm getting the right strain. I isolate the eggs in a tank. By the end of three days, you can see the tiny little eggs, each with two transparent eyes. When they hatch I feed them brine shrimp. At first you can hardly see the fish. I use a magnifying glass. When they're about three weeks of age, I start culling them down for different attributes: color, split fins, anal fins, straight backs and such. It takes a couple of days to get through them all. Out of a hatch of ten thousand eggs, I'm lucky to get fifteen to twenty fish to keep. Out of these, there may be six to twelve good fish. The culls are fed to the other fish. Nothing goes to waste.

You can't tell their sex for about a year. The males have little bumps on the front part of their fins. The females' bellies are softer. I have fish of all ages. A fully developed, good fish is about four years old. Their average life span is five or six years, although some go ten years. At eight years old, my Black Oranda is a granddad.

My dream is to visit a koi farm in Japan some day. Koi live much longer and they're bigger, about twenty-five to twenty-eight inches long. In my ponds, I'm dealing with fish two to six inches long. I keep about a hundred and fifty koi in a pond at Mike Stange's house. To keep them at my place, I'd need an acre to do it right. Mike's gotten real stoked on the koi, and they've become very tame. When Mike swims laps in his pond, the koi follow him.

Some of my fish, especially the ones I've had for years, will come up and eat out of my hand. I don't think they're affectionate, like a dog that eats out of your hand. But they grow to trust you. I can hold my Red Chinese Black Oranda in my hand and he doesn't even wiggle. He knows that I change the water, move the fish around, handle them, feed them. He knows that I'm not going to hurt him. When I'm sitting at the pond to feed my fish and Laura comes out, they all swim away. If Laura sits down in a chair nearby, the fish grudgingly come back over to me for food. They recognize me because I spend so much time with them.

One time, at Kobiyoshi's house in the Islands, I was sitting by one of his ponds, watching fish. There were several other people there, doing the same thing—except for Kobi's wife. She was watching me. She finally approached me, shook her head and said, "Here you are, Greg Noll, a big-wave surfer, watching these little goldfish swim around. I think this is very odd."

I've always had fish tanks and ponds. It's my way of dealing with stress. I can escape from the world and get totally involved in a concentrated, peaceful activity. Sometimes I'll think I've been out there for only ten minutes and then I look at my watch and an hour has gone by.

PURE JOY

When I heard that José Angel had died, a mist went right over my soul. I'm sure all the guys from our time felt the same. Lots of guys have surfed big waves, but only a few of us really enjoyed it. José was one who did.

A few years back, we'd had a couple of lucrative years fishing, so I bought a house on the North Shore to use whenever we were in the Islands. I threw a party there one night and invited José's widow, Moselle, to join us. She lived only a few houses away. I'm sitting there talkin' stories with the Hawaiians when in comes Moe with her kid, Johnny. I just about fell out of my chair. Here is this twelve-year-old boy with José's eyes. A dead ringer for his dad. Moselle said, "Johnny, I want you to meet a friend of your father's." Johnny stuck out his hand and I just grabbed him and gave him a big hug. Made a fool of myself. I don't cry often.

Other Recollections

RICKY GRIGG

José was full of reckless abandon. Physically, he was like a wild man. He had put his life probably closer to the line than any of us ever did, and more often. And yet, José was one who truly surfed for the pure joy of it. In fact, the story of his death might be called "Pure Joy."

Although there was desperation and pressure in his life, you could sense the purity of José's life because he was still living it one day at a time. He had taken on enormous responsibilities. He was supporting two families, one with his first wife, Moselle, and the other with a gal he had recently married. Between them, there were eight kids, and José was in debt. He was diving deep and taking risks to try to catch up with the overbearing pace he had set for himself.

One day during the summer of '76, José went out diving at two hundred and forty feet with Neil Tobin and didn't come up on time. José was decompressing underwater, but Tobin didn't know where he was and he lost him. By the time José did reach the surface, he was a half-mile from the boat and Tobin couldn't find him. José ended up swimming thirteen miles to Molokai.

I came down to the boat one morning about two weeks later. I had been in Washington D.C. on business. José says, "Ricky, I haven't see you for a month! Where have you been? Let's go diving for black coral." We had been partners on Kauai for two and a half years, solid. Campaign after campaign, diving for coral. I dove on the weekends to make extra money, but I also had been studying black coral during the week as part of my regular job. So I said, "What's the plan for the day?"

José told me that he had been diving on a reef at two hundred and forty feet and it was loaded with coral. Since I hadn't been diving for a while, I told José that I'd feel more comfortable diving at one-eighty but not two-forty. He said, "I've just got to do this. I've got orders to fill. Why don't you just come along for the ride?" His thirteen-year-old daughter was also going.

I needed pictures of a diver decompressing for an article I was doing, so I went back to my house to get my camera. I figured I could dive down and meet José as he was decompressing on the way up. He would have to stop at twenty feet and spend about twenty minutes letting out the nitrogen.

So I went out with him with my camera and diving equipment ready. It's a beautiful day, it's calm, there's a rainbow over the cleft in the mountains behind Lahaina, the valley is green and there's rain and mist in the air. As we're going out, José looks back and says, "You know, this is the most beautiful day of my life. I live every day of my life for days like this. I'm going to go out to my favorite place and go for it."

I told him that I wished I was going to be with him on this dive, but it was too deep for me. He said, "That's O.K. No problem. I'm stoked." He was really excited. He was almost vibrating with energy.

168

This was a new place for me, so I rigged up and started getting my camera ready while José and his boatman talked about the lineups. They figure on the spot by using landmarks on shore, in town and on the surrounding hills. The boatman says, "Go!" and José rolls over backward with his float bags and an eighteen-pound sledgehammer tucked into his gut. The weight of the hammer takes you to the bottom real fast, like a shot.

The three of us are in the boat, going around in a circle where José went in. The wind comes up. We're five miles offshore and the wind comes across like a squall. It's blowing fifteen or twenty knots and the sea gets real choppy. There's a lot of glare on the water and we can't see very well. About eleven minutes go by, but José doesn't appear.

Usually we see a float bag after ten minutes, which means the diver is under the bag and is decompressing. Our plan is to go alongside the float bag and I jump in and do the photography. Twelve minutes, no José. Fifteen minutes, and I'm getting panicky. Three minutes is the ballgame out there. If you're off by three minutes, you know something is wrong.

I ask the boatman to put us back on the lineups. I tell him, "I'm going down. Something is wrong." I'm all rigged up, tank and all. We're right smack on the lineups and I take a look at the depthometer. It reads three hundred and sixty feet. I say, "It's three hundred and sixty feet here." The boatman glances at the depthometer and says, "No, it's two-forty." I tell him, "Read the damn thing. It says three-sixty." He looks at it: "Oh, my God. It's on the third scale."

On the second scale, the depth would have been two hundred and forty feet. José had gone off into three hundred and sixty feet of water thinking that it was two-forty.

So, I'm sitting on the edge of the boat, knowing José went to three-sixty and knowing it is physically impossible to survive that depth. His daughter is sitting there and I've got to decide whether I'm going to go down for him, which would be like jumping off the Colony Surf Hotel. I couldn't do it. It's physically impossible to dive to three hundred and sixty feet, much less find someone and bring him up.

I hoped he was downstream, decompressing. That he had got to two hundred and eighty or three hundred feet, realized that he had missed the bottom and dropped his hammer. His depth gauge stopped at two-fifty and he was diving two-forty. If he were to have read it, it would say two-fifty. Since he couldn't have survived beyond that, I figured there

169

was one of two possibilities: he had stopped his descent, dropped his hammer, blown his bags and come up early, or he was lying on the bottom, unconscious, too deep for anyone to find.

We continued on the premise that maybe the float bags had gotten away from him and didn't inflate like they normally do. Maybe he was downstream decompressing. We circled for six hours in ever-widening circles. We got about twenty other boats involved, we called in the Coast Guard, the helicopters. The search lasted three days.

His daughter didn't understand any of what was going on. She kept asking, "What happened, where is my father?" I could have faked it. I could have gone over and gone down to two hundred feet and looked around in the blue. I even thought of going down, just to make her feel like I was doing something under the remote possibility that José was free-floating in the ocean. But I thought the smarter thing to do was to try to find him alive, so we searched downstream.

What I think happened is that he got to two hundred and eighty or three hundred feet and passed out. The top of that coral pinnacle at three hundred and sixty feet was steep. The sides went off four hundred to five hundred feet. José just went off into the deep blue.

———————————

TURNING POINT

I had just come back to the shop after having lunch with a friend when Beverly came running out and said, "You'd better get over to your mom's house."

I went there right away. My father was lying on the floor. An ambulance had just arrived. He'd had a heart attack. They took him to the hospital and that was it.

He was only fifty-five and had never been seriously ill. I was thirty-four. He had been a big force in my life. He was always calm, pleasant. All the good things you could ever think to say about someone, you could say about my dad, Ash Noll. Laura and I named our daughter, Ashlyne, after him.

He and my mom had another son, Jimmy. Jimmy took after my father. Very easygoing. It's interesting to me that, even though they're not blood-related, my oldest son, Tate, picked up a lot of my dad's and Jimmy's attributes. Tate's a free and easy, good-hearted kid who loves life. All my kids have one thing in common. They've all been on a surfboard before the age of four.

I took Jimmy surfing almost before he could walk. He still remembers the time I took him to Malibu. We rode a wave together, all the way from the Point. He was such a little fart that when I grabbed his hands to help him stand up, he came right up off the board.

My father's death was the beginning of some real problems for me, for about three years afterwards. That was when I started taking a different look at my life.

MIKE STANGE

The death of his stepfather was the hardest thing that Greg ever had to go through. I took Greg up to Crescent City to do a little fishing, just to get him away from everything. I had been up there before, fishing with my dad and brother, and I knew Greg would take to it.

We didn't know anything about salmon fishing. Greg figured it out, though. That's how it always was with us, whether surfing or fishing. I'd go along, and Greg would figure out the details. And we'd always have fun together.

For months after my father's death, I couldn't function around people. I didn't want to be around anyone. I had never enjoyed being in large rooms full of people. I'm pretty comfortable in a one-on-one situation, but I have trouble when people are milling around in a crowd.

I remember going to industry functions, like the Surfer Poll banquet. I'd drink to hide my tension and then would always end up getting shit-faced, wishing I could escape. Just a few years ago, I took my kids to one of Dewey Weber's longboard contests in the South Bay. I thought we might just slide into the crowd and watch the contest. We weren't there for five minutes when I hear this announcement come over the P.A. system: "Ladies and gentlemen, may I have your attention." My skin just started to crawl. I knew it was coming. "If you will focus your attention on the pier . . . " I just grabbed my kids and took off.

After that day at Big Makaha in '69, I made a few more trips to the Islands. I'd surf, but not with the same drive or intensity. Whenever I'd go to an area where there were a bunch of surfers, I'd try to avoid them. But, there was one occasion when I actually enjoyed the recognition I got.

I had driven my family to a surf spot on the windy side of the Big Island of Hawaii. I parked about fifty yards away from where a group of surfers were standing and got out of the car to watch the other guys in the water. After a few minutes I noticed a guy walking up a path towards me, carrying his board. He was just kickin' along until he got about ten feet in front of me. He looked up and stopped. I saw that look of recognition come across his face. I thought, "Oh shit, here it comes, twenty minutes of 'How's it feel to ride Big Waimea?' " Instead he just said, "Are you . . . ?" And I said yes. He said, "I thought so." As he walked by, I put my hand out, he shook it and then continued walking. That guy had a lot of class.

Some of the most memorable times of my life have occurred while surfing with a half-dozen other guys at Waimea Bay or Sunset Beach. All of us sharing and enjoying the energy. At Sunset Beach in the afternoon, the wind blows out of the valley and holds up the waves. You'd paddle out and hear one of the guys shout, "Yeeeooow!" as he took off on a nice, crisp wave. It's hard to explain how fun and holy these times were. Put a couple of goddamn cameras on the beach, turn it into a contest, set up bleachers and the whole thing goes to shit.

We'd all gather at the Seaview Inn in Haleiwa after a day of surfing Waimea. Maybe Buzzy, Peter, Ricky and I, rehashing our rides, relaxing. Suddenly, in comes a couple of magazine writers, a couple of photographers. Then the bullshit begins, the whole scene gets tense and goes to shit again.

I try to figure out why I react to certain things in certain ways, but I never figured out why I reacted the way I did to my father's death. How do you come to understand how a good person can suddenly be gone? And what's the point of trying to figure it out anyway? People have been trying to figure out that one since the beginning of time.

During this same time, I also had become fed up with the whole Southern California scene. It was 1971 and the surf scene was turning, getting crowded. Everything I had known as a young man was turning to shit. So when my father died, I started doing some serious thinking, like "What's the big deal about blindly working your ass off, trying to make a lot of money and screwing the next guy before he screws you?"

After Mike Stange and I returned from our fishing trip to Crescent City, I started thinking, "Maybe I could turn this thing around and spend more time with my family, my kids, and enjoy a little bit of the nature that God put on this earth." Manhattan Beach, Hermosa and L.A. just didn't have it for me anymore.

BEVERLY

Ash was truly a father to Greg. Greg and I were married for years before I ever knew that there was any other father besides Ash. You meet a lot of people in your life, but you can count maybe only a few who really touch your life. Ash was someone who touched me. He was very, very special to me.

Ash was a very easy man, a quiet man. Didn't have a whole lot to say, but when he said something, you'd listen. His eyes sparkled. He was so reserved that when he smiled only the very corner of his mouth would turn up. But his eyes just danced. A lovely, lovely man.

Ash's death happened at a time when everything else was coming down. The business was on its way out. We were in the process of withdrawing but we couldn't withdraw quickly enough, with the decline of the surf business and the economy. Ash was probably the only stable factor in Greg's life. His death marked the finality of anything that Greg had a grip on at that time.

SONNY VARDEMAN

The business going under and Ash's death were tremendous blows to Greg. He retreated. I mean, he was in full retreat. He withdrew from his friends, got an unlisted phone number. His aggressive nature re-appeared. He'd be in a bar and someone would give him a cross-eyed look and he'd go after them. He had a lot of anger in him. You still see it in him now and then.

I didn't see him for a couple of years. I had some of my own personal and business problems to deal with — a divorce and the closing of my own surfboard business in Huntington Beach that I'd had for ten years. A lot of guys who we'd grown up with went under during the early seventies.

After my father's death, I went back to the beach and worked as a lifeguard for the summer. Sat in the tower on my section of the beach. Most of the time it was quiet. Nobody bothered me. Laura would come out every afternoon and go over business. She took care of the shop while I sat out there.

I felt like a kid, going off into a corner to suck on my thumb. Lifeguarding is a far cry from running a surf shop with sixty-five employees. From that point on, things got very peaceful for me. I just couldn't listen to another stoked kid with another surf story or listen to some "neat idea" for a new board that I had already built twenty-five times over the years. You can't feel that way and run a successful business. I became rude. I was burned-out and didn't give a goddamn any more.

The man wearing a suit in the ads, the fancy office, the ocelot—none of that was me. The real me was a pretty boring guy. I just wanted to find someplace quiet where I could enjoy my family, play with the kids, swim in the ocean and do some hunting and fishing. All the other stuff was a means of playing the game, playing along to make money, to get ahead, to do whatever it is society tells you to do to succeed. I finally decided, piss on that. It wasn't worth the pretense. Time to get back to the adage "If it feels good, do it."

I was surfed- and storied-out. We decided to liquidate the shop. Beverly took on that task while Laura and I took off for Alaska to look for a new way of life.

ALASKA-BOUND

LAURA

Greg had been caught up in a tremendous roll. For a long time, everything he did worked. Everything made money. It just kept building and building and he kept going and going. Then it stopped. The business went sour and Ash died. Greg never came back to the shop after that.

Alaska had been a fantasy to us. We had heard tales of huge salmon, wild animals, beautiful country, log cabins and no people. We had made several trips to Crescent City over the years, fishing and drifting the Smith River, and it only heightened our enthusiasm to see Alaska.

We bought an old delivery van and converted it into a motorhome. It contained just about everything we needed for cold or heat, hunting, fishing, drifting, hiking or canning salmon. We were prepared, and our van looked like it. We were so excited and full of anticipation of what this unknown country might have in store for us.

Laura and I brought along her dog, Al, and stayed in Alaska for three months. We almost got ourselves in a heap of trouble on one part of that trip. We had decided to drift a section of the Kispiox River. In five days, we covered a thirty-mile stretch that had never been drifted before. Half

176

the time we didn't know where we were. We drifted through some giant, deep canyons. The river had risen above many of the landmarks that we could have used to find our position. We had driven upriver from a lodge to start the trip. When we showed up back at the lodge five days later, the locals couldn't believe that we actually had made it.

At one place we set up camp on an island. The river had begun to swell from a big rain. During the night, the river continued to rise and the island started to disappear. That's when we discovered that we had been sharing the island with a bear. I had gone out to pull the boat farther up on the sand, and saw this bear down the beach, looking for a way off the island. Later, in the middle of the night, we heard him dive off the bank and into the water. It wasn't long afterwards that Laura, Al and I also had to abandon the island. The river eventually covered it over.

The journey wasn't what the word "drift" implies. By that time, the river was raging, the rain was falling in sheets and we could hardly see beyond the bow of the boat. I pulled up under a clump of trees that was still above water, tied off the boat and tried to rest until daylight.

We barely slept. At dawn, we discovered that we had stopped only a couple hundred feet before a giant logjam that was sucking the water underneath it. Had we gone up against that in the middle of the night, we'd have dumped the boat for sure and been pulled underwater to drown.

Other times, we had to get out and drag the boat across marshy ground. Drifting that section of the Kispiox wasn't the smartest thing I had ever done, but we had some incredible encounters with animals and saw some spectacular country.

Alaska is the place to see wildlife. One day we came around a curve by a stream and saw an eagle diving down, raking his feet across the water in pursuit of a fish. Another time, we were camped up in the woods on the night of a full moon and a bear woke us up in the middle of the night. He was fooling around with the tailpipe on the van. I had visions of a bear rug, so I grabbed an old .308 that I had brought along and peeked into the rearview mirror to get a fix on the bugger. Then I opened the window as quickly as I could, stuck out the rifle and got off a shot that lit up the whole sky. I don't know who was more scared, me or the bear. The poor guy rolled over about three times, then all I saw was ass and fur flying down the road. I had missed him. All this time, Al is going crazy barking.

177

I don't know if my rifle caused it, but that night the whole mountain we were camped under gave way. We thought we were going to be buried in an avalanche. When it let go, it sounded like thunder. I figured we were as safe in the van as anywhere, so we just sat tight. Fortunately, the avalanche came down quite a ways from us.

We went up into the glaciated high country and met some of the most radical guys I've ever met in my life. They were loggers—rough, hard-drinking outdoor types. They congregated at an old bar in Hyder. Stuck all over the walls were cards from people who had been to the bar during the past few decades. We got "Hyder-ized" at this bar by tossing down a shot of hundred-and-fifty-proof corn liquor, all in one gulp, an initiation that all newcomers had to undergo.

One of the guys in the bar took a shine to us. His name was Lenny. He had been hunting the week before in an area that was being logged and had bagged himself a beautiful shaggy-furred mountain goat that had enormous horns. I was so stoked by his story that he offered to take me and Laura there.

After six hours of hiking, we hit steep terrain. Lenny asked Laura to wait on a ridge while he and I scouted ahead. A little ways on, he told me to wait at a certain trail near our camp while he followed some hot tracks. While I was waiting, I spotted where the tracks split and went off the other way. There were fresh droppings where the goat had just been. I decided not to wait for Lenny and I took off, following the tracks along a trail that ended at the edge of a steep cliff.

Man, you think looking over the edge into the pit of a thirty-foot grinder at Waimea makes your toes curl, you should try looking over the edge of a bottomless pit. I crawled up to the edge of the cliff on my belly, sweating every inch, then pushed a couple of good-sized rocks over and waited several endless seconds before I heard a faint, far-off crash. I inched closer to the edge and found myself looking straight down a few thousand feet of sheer granite rock face. It took my breath away. Instead of the adrenalin rush that comes with a Waimea elevator-drop takeoff, all I felt was cold fear. I've never been so goddamned scared in my life. I started backing away from the edge on my hands and knees, dragging my beautiful Browning V, my pride and joy, through the dirt with visions of that whole cliff collapsing under me.

I happened to glance up and notice that one part of the trail led out onto a granite ledge. And there he was, his tail pointed towards me, twitching. I could have shot him, but there was no way I could have gotten him back to camp. I whispered, "You win, buddy," and carefully made my way back to Laura and our guide, Lenny.

STORMS AT SEA

Alaska is an incredibly beautiful place that leaves such a strong impression on you that you want to run out and tell somebody about it. The impression is so strong that as soon as you leave, the whole experience starts to fade, like a dream. All that's left is a feeling, deep down inside, of knowing that you'll go back someday.

Eventually, we sold off everything that had to do with the surfboard business. I kept all my templates and tools, but the rest of the inventory was sold off. Then I piled the family and our worldly possessions into our old Metro van and off we went to Crescent City to start a new life.

Before we got into commercial fishing, I spent some time running with some local hunters and fishermen. Wore my plaid shirt and sawed-off logger's pants with suspenders. I got to be a real Northwest-type guy. It was something new to do. Something that didn't involve Greg Noll, Big-Wave Surfer.

Commercial fishing is a big business in Crescent City. We knew it involved a big financial commitment. But like everything else, we just went into it headlong. Within three years, we had a full-on operation. It worked out to where Beverly and I ran the boat while Laura ran the support system on shore, overseeing all the details for marketing the catch.

When we first moved to Crescent City, we had no idea that we would get into commercial fishing. We had a skiff and we'd just go out fishing. One day I caught a big salmon, and a light went on in my head: "We could make a living at this." We got our license and started fishing salmon commercially from a little, twenty-four-foot boat. We did pretty well that year, so the next year we bought a little bigger boat and started fishing for crab. That year happened to bring one of the biggest crab seasons ever. Before then, crab had been flat for about six years. It's usually impossible for a newcomer to get a crab market, but a friend of ours, Kenny Butler, who manages Eureka Fisheries, gave me crab market, which gave us the ability to sell crab.

We started with ten crab pots, put them out at South Beach and the things were plugged in no time. We worked up to seventy-five pots that year, ended up paying for the boat and had a little left over. We were stoked.

The following year, we bought a forty-two-foot boat, the *Della*. We fished off the *Della* for three or four years, then went off the deep end with the *Ashlyne,* a 65-foot steel-hulled boat that had a hundred-and-ten-ton fish hold. We named it after my daughter. It was a giant boat. And it put us right back into what we were running away from. Giant crew. Giant business. We had to make over two hundred thousand dollars a year just to meet payments and payroll. Life's weird, isn't it? So for the next ten years, I'm bobbing around on the ocean, day and night.

There's something to do on the boat year-round. You start fishing shrimp in April or May and go through September. You also get swordfish permits, so if your shrimp fizzles out, you can throw out the gill nets and go for swordfish. Then you get ready for crab season, which begins in December and usually goes through February.

As a surfer, I saw some pretty incredible things happen out on the ocean. As a commercial fisherman, I've seen surf and conditions that would turn just about any surfer I know goddamn white. I've seen more guys killed in commercial fishing than I ever saw or would have seen while surfing. Only difference is, in fishing, there are no cameras, no audiences.

Commercial fishing is recognized by insurance companies as one of the most hazardous of all occupations. In fifteen years of fishing, I've lost at least one close friend a year. In one instance, it was the guy who had the slip right next to mine. For three years, we had traded tools, fished together, shared information. We were buddies. A couple of years ago, he and his three boys were making their last trip of the year before the boys had to go back to school. Now they're gone, without a trace of them or their boat.

181

Another guy two slips over from mine lost his boat in Alaska. There were five guys on the boat. They were anchored up in some bay and woke up in the middle of the night with their stern end underwater. The galley was going down first so they went topside into the pilothouse, but the boat was laid over to starboard on the door. The only way out was through the portholes. Four of the guys managed to squeeze through, but the fifth guy was too big and couldn't get out. His last words were "Take care of the family for me." Then he went down with the boat in six fathoms of water.

One of the best and most successful fishermen in the harbor had five boats and a multimillion-dollar operation. Nicest guy you'd ever want to meet. Coming off a trip, about fifteen minutes out of the harbor, he popped a sinker rock in the middle of the night and the boat went down. His deck hand was also a surfer. He managed to get to the beach, but he was so cold and full of water that he died in the hospital. They didn't find the skipper's body until four days later.

In surfing, if somebody drowns or gets killed in the surf, it's a big deal. In commercial fishing here in the north country, if a guy does down, it's the talk of the dock for a few days, then it's business as usual. It's not that people don't care. They know it's something they have to live with.

At Waimea, twenty-foot ground swells at sea generally produce close-out surf in the Bay. In the winter of '87, we fished out of Westport, Washington, near Grays Harbor. We just barely got in from one storm that produced thirty-four-foot ground swells. These are accurate measurements. Not a couple of guys sitting on the point above Waimea with a six-pack, bullshitting about how big the waves are. I had laid a hundred and four crab pots at fifteen fathoms, or ninety feet deep. After that storm subsided, we came back out and found that we had lost most of our gear. I had a plotter on the boat that laid out an exact line so you can retrieve your pots. These pots weighed anywhere from seventy-five to a hundred pounds each. Out of those hundred and four we found six. A few of them were four miles away from where they had been laid. The rest were just gone. It's hard to imagine the size and force of the waves that did this.

These are gut-grinding situations. A surfer out in big surf has only himself to be concerned about. As a skipper, you're responsible for your vessel and crew. I think my years on the ocean, surfing, enabled me to get into commercial fishing very quickly and to read and survive some situations that otherwise would have taken a long time to learn.

The weather reports that you get at sea are broken into areas along the coast by the National Weather Service reports. You get one report from the Crescent City area, which fades off at Fort Bragg, where you pick up another that goes from Fort Bragg to Point Reyes. Then you pick up another that goes from Point Reyes to Half Moon Bay, and so on.

We almost ate it one time, coming back up the coast from Morro Bay. We had just finished fishing off Avila and were on our way home. Just as we were coming around Point Reyes, something felt strange to me. I was getting a weather report on the VHF that said fifteen-knot winds variable, no sweat. But there was this cross swell coming around Point Reyes and it went flat dead calm and it just felt goofy to me.

I decided to call home through the marine operator to another friend of mine who was fishing on the land line. I said to him, "Harry, what's going on? The weather doesn't feel right down here." He said, "Turn that sonofabitch around right now and head it for the barn. We've got hundred-knot winds offshore. Everything is cinched down in the harbor and the flagpole at the park is bent over." The storm was moving south in our direction. We were in the kick-back, the calm before the storm.

If we had gone north, beyond Point Reyes, we'd have had no place to tuck in. The *Ashlyne* drew nine feet, four inches, so we'd have drug ass trying to get into the next port, Bodega Bay, and would have ended up losing her on the beach. We'd have never made it to the harbor at Fort Bragg—it would have been closed out by then.

I switched radio channels and heard the tankers a hundred miles north of me bitching that they were getting eighty-knot winds on the outside, gusting to ninety. When those guys squawk, you know you've got troubles coming. So we flipped her around and started in, back to San Francisco Bay.

We only had a twelve-mile run to San Francisco Bay. We got about four miles and the wind hit hard. We headed down the slot, a deep channel about three hundred feet wide where you can sneak between the land mass and a narrow reef that's called the Potato Patch. Supposedly, the Potato Patch got its name from all the old-time boats that carried big loads of potatoes. When it got rough enough on that reef, the potatoes would roll off as their ships made for port.

It was about three in the morning and the wind was now blowing at sixty or seventy knots. It was raining and blowing like a sonofabitch, and off the starboard side it looked like Waimea Bay. Huge waves were breaking on the Potato Patch, rolling across the reef and dissipating right at the edge of the deep channel, just yards from us. We could hardly see, and the radar was going haywire because she was rolling so badly. Up ahead, on the inside, we could see whitewater hitting the cliffs and spraying three hundred feet into the air.

The *Ashlyne* was a lot of boat and took a lot of weather, but she was like a little toy bobbing around that day. We almost lost her. Up ahead, I could just see the Golden Gate Bridge, but I couldn't find the buoy that marked the next part of the reef. We inched our way along. I finally spotted a little hook-and-line boat up ahead. He was a local fisherman and knew the area. We followed him in. As we entered the harbor, Beverly and I both remarked that the Golden Gate Bridge had never looked better.

When you get under that bridge, the wind can really haul. But at that point, you're out of danger of the surf or of hitting the reefs. That night she blew so hard that five boats were lost outside San Francisco Bay. By morning, it was blowing a hundred knots on the outside. We were locked in the bay for a week while the storm blew itself out. By the end, a dozen boats had been lost at sea with their crews, and many more had been damaged.

Another time we got into a southerly. I came around Mendocino and took a straight bearing for Crescent City. The storm was on our ass and we were just smoking along. There were down-swells, the wind was blowing close to fifty and the rain started pouring down. Suddenly we hit the center. I've never done this before or since, or come close to anything like it. We actually were in the eye of the storm.

Behind us we could see ground swells and fifteen-foot whitecaps. In front of us we could see the same thing coming at us from about a mile away. The air was dead calm where we sat, but the water was as turbulent as a washing machine. Eerie as hell. I had to manually steer the Sperry auto pilot because the compass was spinning around in circles.

I called the Coast Guard and asked for their weather report. They were giving small-craft warnings. I told them I would like the guy who wrote that goddamn report to be sitting in my pilot house taking a look out my window. My wind meter had registered sixty knots.

BEVERLY

That time we came across the Potato Patch was the only time I've been scared out on the ocean. Greg and I were the only crew on the boat. I had just come off a long watch and had gone below to get some sleep. Greg came down and shook me awake, saying, "Bev, you'd better come up here."

I dragged myself up to the pilothouse and Greg says, "Something is wrong." I'm listening to the engine, which sounds fine, and looking out at the water, which looks glassy. Everything seemed O.K. to me. But Greg said, "This swell is coming from someplace and I don't like it." That's when we called up north.

As we headed down the slot, we could barely see the mast light on the little hook-and-line boat up ahead. I crawled out the door on my hands and knees around the front shield, and used the hand wiper to keep the window clean for Greg. It was a traumatic experience, going into a strange harbor at night during a raging storm. These things always seem to happen at night.

When we moved to Crescent City, I didn't even know what commercial fishing was. Our idea was to bail out of Southern California and get into a clean way of living to raise the kids. We originally thought we'd go to Alaska and live in the back hills. Crescent City was supposed to have been just a pit stop.

A friend of mine, Billy Robinson, once asked to ride back up the coast with me from San Pedro to Crescent City. He was a lifeguard and also competed in Ironman triathlons. Hell of an athlete. Before we left the harbor at San Pedro he asked me, "Do you ever get any water up here on the bridge?" The bridge on the Ashlyne stood almost eighteen feet off the water. I said, "Oh yeah, sometimes." He decided to bring his wetsuit, face plate and fins with him just in case.

As you go up the California Coast, each point you pass takes on a different, more ominous look. Compared to the northern coast, the

185

southern coast is like the Bahamas. Then you get up off San Francisco and around Point Reyes and the coast takes on a different twist. The biggest change occurs at Mendocino. When you go around the spark plug there at Mendocino, you're in the north country and it's a whole different program.

We'd been underway all night. By the time Billy came up out of the rack, it had kicked up good. The wind had blown all night. It was a close storm and moving in on us fast. We were going into troughs twenty-to-twenty-five-feet deep. You couldn't see out either side when the boat dropped into one of those. So here comes Billy, wiping the sleepers out of his eyes just as we punched into the bottom of one of these troughs. Tons of spray buried the bow, flew completely over the bridge and down behind the boat. I said, "Hey, Billy, remember when you asked if we ever get any water up here?"

He glanced over at his wetsuit and fins. I said, "It isn't going to do you any good. If something happens to the boat out here, do yourself a favor and jump over the side, let all your air out and just get it over with as quickly as you can." Billy made some comment about how comforting it was to have such a reassuring skipper.

Everything went great with our fishing operation until my attention span started to fade. My motivation really came more from the challenge of figuring out the mechanics of commercial fishing, understanding the nets, the electronics and all. Once I had brought all this together and made a successful business of it, the challenge disappeared.

Bev and I found ourselves going in different directions. She wanted to keep the boat and I wanted out. Being on the ocean together for long periods of time in a confined space can be tough on relationships. A lot of tension built up between Beverly and me and just tore us apart.

I had stuck with it for fifteen years, about twice as long as I originally had thought I would when we got the boat. During the last few years it evolved to Beverly taking out the boat and my helping out with technical aspects, until I got out of the business altogether. Eventually, the boat was sold.

Beverly's a hell of an individual. She's the only woman I know who ever captained a sixty-five-foot steel-hulled fishing boat on this entire coast, including Alaska.

Our situation also evolved to my spending more time with Laura. We had two young children, Ashlyne and Jed, who needed my attention.

As I grew older, I became more entrenched with my "new" family. I still have strong family ties with Bev and our boys, Tate and Rhyn, but I've found that I want to be with Laura. So Beverly and I finally went our separate ways. We still get together for family occasions. Laura and Bev are still friends, and all the kids are close. What always has made our situation work was not me, but Laura and Bev. They're both extraordinary individuals. That's why they were able to cope with such an unusual situation.

Other Recollections

LAURA

Very few people really know or understand Greg. Mike Stange is one person and I'd like to think that I am another, but sometimes I wonder. Greg never will be content. He goes at everything with a vengeance and doesn't stop until he knows all there is to know. Someone once said, "Greg goes about things like he's killing snakes."

He's changed from his early days of surfing and pulling pranks and is surprised that people remember him. In Crescent City and to Ashlyne and Jed, he's just another fisherman and their dad. As the kids grow older, they learn more about what he accomplished in the surfing world and are awed when other people recognize him.

Greg's reputation has not always been the best, but in a way, he's used his hell-raising adventures to hide the real Greg Noll. He's a very caring person, but reserves this side of himself for the people closest to him. He's still full of adventure and talks of Australia and New Zealand the way we used to talk about Alaska. I often wonder what other fantasies will become reality in our life together.

THE GREEN ROOM

If people really want to know what surfing big waves is all about, they should get a board and go out there. Or sit on the beach and watch it, get the smell and feel of it while it's happening. It's like watching an Indy driver set speed records or watching a mountain climber plant his ice ax on the summit of Everest. There's no bullshit involved in doing these things. The bullshit comes when you start the endorsements, selling backpacks used on Everest, the A. J. Foyt tires, Da Bull's striped trunks. That's all bullshit, and I've been a part of it just like everyone else.

I don't deny that making money is part of life. There's just less bullshit involved when you're free to make a commitment to something pure, like riding a big wave. Drop the nose of your board down that face, take a few strokes and you're "coming down," as Georgie Downing would say when he took off on a grinder at Makaha or Waimea. And if you hesitate or you find you don't have the balls to battle with the thing, well, that's part of coming to grips with the nitty-gritty side of life.

To me, what I did at Waimea and at Makaha is not spectacular. I devoted myself to surfing big waves. I worked up to it and ended up being comfortable with something that a lot of guys tried to achieve and didn't. To me, that didn't make it spectacular. I simply worked my way up to it. Just as a race-car driver or a mountain climber would do. You don't win the big race or reach the summit the first time out.

I've screwed up a lot in my life. But there are certain things I am proud of. I'm proud to have pioneered Waimea Bay and to have introduced the modern-day surfboard to Australia. I'm proud to have a watch inscribed to me from Duke Kahanamoku. I'm proud of the fact that I took a young Buffalo Keaulana to town one day and helped contribute to his development as an informal statesman for Hawaii. I'm proud to have Buff, Henry and Mike Stange as brothers. I'm proud to have served as a lifeguard with my lifelong friends from the South Bay. And I'm proud to have such a loving family.

There's something else. I looked up my real father a few years ago. I hadn't seen him for forty-five years and I was curious. I discovered that he had followed my career. He told me that before he retired and moved farther south, he had a home in Malibu. There he got to know a lot of surfers who told him all about Greg Noll. Now we see him whenever we go to Southern California. The kids go swimming in the surf near his house and they love him. I do, too.

When I was three years old, I almost drowned. My mom had taken me over to a friend's house. They went inside to talk while I stayed outside to play around a big, deep fish pond in the backyard. As Mom tells it, she looked out the window to check on me and all she saw was a blond tuft of hair, floating on the surface of the fish pond.

I wasn't breathing when my mom and her friend hauled me out of the pond, but they managed to bring me around. Mom says that, as soon as I recovered I was ready to go back in again. That was my first experience over the edge. And my first reprieve.

Other Recollections

FRED HEMMINGS
1968 World Surfing Champion, Hawaii State Legislator

Greg Noll was a modern-day mountain man like the legendary characters of the Rockies during the days of the Wild West. He was a rough, tough guy. Not the kind of guy you would find eating quiche. He drank hard, played hard, did not take lip from anybody and he rode big waves. Greg Noll will be remembered as one of the special breed of surfers who pioneered big-wave riding.

Big-wave surfing has not changed much down through the years. I do not believe that many surfers understand some of the dynamics and physical limitations inherent in big-wave surfing. Basically, the larger the wave, the faster the water races up the face of the wave. In really large surf, the water moving up the face of the wave is moving faster than the surfer's ability to paddle into the wave. The surfer gets sucked to the top of the wave until it becomes so steep that he falls down the face. The odds of maintaining control during the drop-in on real large surf are such that surfers are not really riding waves, they are just plummeting out of control down the face of a mountain of water. There is a big difference between "drop-in daredevils" and accomplished big-wave riders.

Excitement for many is found on the edge. Many of life's greatest challenges are found in one's own mind or are self-imposed obstacles. Big waves certainly are a physical and mental challenge. In really large surf, fear is a major factor.

That day at Makaha in '69 happened during an epic week of twenty-foot surf. The morning of the biggest day found several surfers, including Rolf Aurness, Charlie Galanto and myself, stroking out into what was easily twenty-five-foot-plus surf. Personally, I was as scared as I have ever been, so scared that while sitting on the Point I was tempted to paddle to Waianae to get in safely. I did ride a rather large wave. Now, years later, it's easy to admit I did not go out for more because I was scared. On that day you would wait a half-hour or so to pick your wave. In surf like that you feel that a mistake could cost you your life.

Greg Noll had paddled out. All of us were on shore as he finally stroked into a wave that filled the whole horizon. It really was the biggest wave I believe anyone had ever caught. It was a death-wish wave. He elevator-dropped to the bottom. The wave broke over him. The entire ocean seemed to be moving toward the shore. He came up and eventually made it to the beach. I think he was glad to be alive. I *know* he was lucky to be alive.

That day at Big Makaha was like looking goddamn flat over the edge at the big, black pit. Some of my best friends have said that it was a death-wish wave. I didn't feel that way at the time, but in retrospect I realize that it probably was bordering on the edge. To have pushed beyond that would have been a death wish.

I love the Islands and I love the Hawaiian people. I envy Ricky and Peter, still surfing the North Shore and Makaha. For me this option doesn't exist. For me it has to be all or nothing.

In my mind, I never quit surfing. Surfing is a feeling that never leaves you. I'm still a part of the ocean. I've just turned my attention to other challenges. In fifteen years of commercial fishing, I spent more concentrated time on the ocean than I ever spent surfing. I'm just looking at the same deal from another angle.

In many ways, I'm still that twelve-year-old boy surfing at Manhattan Beach Pier. I'm restless, I'm ready to see new places. I think about Australia now and then. If I could find a little secluded beach, a pretty little reef to dive and enough waves to go Poipu-boarding with the kids, that would be fine.

But I could never live in the Islands. It tortures me today to turn on the TV and see Big Waimea and not be a part of it. I turn it off. Or if Laura and the kids are watching, I'll pace outside. I'll sneak in for a peek now and then, bitch about the way they're doing something with the boards these days, then go outside and pace some more. I can't sit there and watch it, knowing that I'm no longer a part of it. It drives me nuts and it would drive me nuts to live in the Islands.

To me the Islands are like an eternally beautiful woman. I'm growing older but she's still this neat little gal I can remember making love to when I was young. She never changes, but I do.

NO BULL

RICKY GRIGG

There are still places and times when it's timeless. There are mornings here in Hawaii when there is only one other guy out in the water. It could be 1952 or it could be now. It's like that at Waimea once in a while, usually when the contests are someplace else.

When I look at my whole life of surfing, I know I haven't ridden as many waves as Greg has, even now. I never was surfing full time, except for three years between stints in college. Nor was Peter. I think one reason Peter and I have not burned out is because we're still catching up to Greg and the guys who were out there all the time. Usually Peter and I couldn't get out in the water until late afternoon, and then we'd have to quit a couple hours later, unsatiated. The essence of the sport to us right now is that we are still unsatiated. We go surfing four, maybe five times a month.

Most people who have excelled in this sport have done it in intense periods of time. Then they have gone off to do other things. Peter and I are not as competitive as we once were. When surfing is just recreation, you never get tired of it.

The worst thing about my job as an oceanographer is being with people who don't have the heart to understand the ocean from the perspective that Greg, Peter and I do. When you can join hands with the Greg Nolls and the Peter Coles of the world, you experience something that is often lacking in other people who have dedicated their professional

192

lives to the ocean. As a surfer and a commercial fisherman, Greg under-stands the storms, the interaction of weather, temperature and currents and how they affect his resource. He's a man of the ocean who has been out there struggling to produce. It's been his life, his sustenance, his recreation, his drama, his job, his heart. Everything is wound up with this thing in an emotional way. You take an oceanographer, sitting there with a computer and a map and telling you how the Coriolis force works and you couldn't care less.

I feel a strong influence on my thinking from being out on the ocean alone and having to make decisions regarding my survival, right then and there. It's like living in a different society, where you make up rules as the need arises. What strikes me as amazing is that there are departments at colleges and universities where we teach people about the ocean and there's no hands-on stuff. Greg has told me that most commercial fisher-men can't swim. The same is true of most oceanographers. They are totally inept in the element in which they spend most of their professional lives.

I used to feel that there was a lot of hype put on big-wave surfing, but I don't feel that way anymore. I feel it's a real thing; it's so valid that we can't do it justice with words. When surfing was first coming of age in the fifties and sixties, all of us were riding a wave of popularity and saying, "Yeah, yeah, we're gladiators," and all that. As it turned out, there is no bullshit. Lifting off on those waves, it *is* a moment of truth.

The heart of the story about our years of surfing is the emotion we share. It's like old bullfighters getting together. What's important is not how fast the bull is running; it's how it feels when he misses you by an inch. That's the story, isn't it?

ACKNOWLEDGMENTS

The authors wish to extend their appreciation to the various people who took the time to contribute their energy and recollections to this book. Specifically: Beverly and Laura, Duke Boyd, Ken Bradshaw, Bruce Brown, Bud Browne, Gordon "Grubby" Clark, Peter Cole, Mike Doyle, Richard Graham, Leroy Grannis, Ricky Grigg, Fred Hemmings, Tak Kawahara, Buffalo Keaulana, Dick Metz, Sam Moses, Henry Preece, Michael Stange, Eddie Talbot, Sonny Vardeman and Dale Velzy. Special thanks to Marlene Alsko for transcripts, to Brad Bonhall for copy editing, to Kelly Culwell and Patricia Sullivan for word-processing assistance, to Cindy Love for art direction, to Jerry Newton for photographic work, to *Surfer* magazine for photographs, to Allan Seymour for guidance and promotional efforts, to our patient and supportive families and friends. Last, a heartfelt thanks to our mentor and Greg's silent fishing partner, who shall remain unnamed but not forgotten.